OSHO

A New Vision of Women's Liberation

FULL CIRCLE

A NEW VISION OF WOMEN'S LIBERATION

Originally published by: The Rebel Publishing House,
West Germany, under the author name Bhagwan Shree Rajneesh

Co-ordination by : Amano Surdham
New Edition, 2004
First Reprint, 2006
Reprinted with New Layout, 2011
This Reprint, May 2019

ISBN 13: 978-81-7621-160-4

For Sale in India only

Published by **FULL CIRCLE PUBLISHING** *PVT LTD*
J-40, Jorbagh Lane, New Delhi-110003
Tel: +011-24621011
E-mail: contact@fullcirclebooks.in *website:* www.fullcirclebooks.in

Typesetting: SCANSET
J-40, Jorbagh Lane, New Delhi-110003

Printed at Yash Printographics, C-37, Sector-58, Noida-201301 U.P.

PRINTED IN INDIA

A New Vision of Women's Liberation

OSHO FROM FULL CIRCLE

- Gita Darshan (Vol-II)
- Gita Darshan (Vol-I)
- Tao: The Pathless Path
- Inner War and Peace
- Die O' Yogi Die
- Behind A Thousand Names
- Freedom from the Past
- Ah This!
- The Way of the Sufi
- The Silence of the Heart
- The True Name
- The Secret
- Truth Simply Is
- In Search of Celebration
- From Sex to Superconsciousness
- Never Born, Never Died
- Walk without feet, Fly without wings...
- Won't you Join the Dance?
- Priests & Politicians – The Mafia of the Soul
- My Diamond Days with Osho
- Tantra – The Supreme Understanding
- The Goose is Out
- Sex, Money and Power
- The Rebel
- A New Vision of Women's Liberation
- I Teach Religiousness Not Religion
- Words From A Man of No Words
- First In The Morning
- Last In The Evening

Contents

Part I

CHAPTER 1

If You Don't Know What You Are Missing...

I have heard You say that ninety-eight percent of the women of the East have not known orgasm. Why is it they look so graceful and not frustrated like the women in the West?

It is a strange logic of life, but in a way very simple. In the East, ninety-eight percent of the women have not known what orgasm is. Your question is, "Why is it they look so graceful and not frustrated like the women in the West?" That's why! You have to be in a position of experiencing something and then having it denied to you; only then frustration sets in. If you don't know at all that anything like orgasm exists, then there is no question of frustration. In the West also, before this century, the woman was not frustrated, because the situation was the same there.

It was because of psychoanalysis and the deeper researches into human energies that it was discovered that, for a millennium, we have lived under a fallacy. The fallacy was that the woman has a vaginal orgasm, which has not been found to be true; she does not have a vaginal orgasm at all.

In fact, the woman's vagina is absolutely insensitive, it feels nothing. Her orgasm is clitoral – and that is a totally separate part. She can reproduce children without knowing any orgasm, she can make love without knowing any orgasm. Hence for centuries, in the East and West both, the woman was satisfied to become a mother. In a way she was against sex, because it was not giving her any joy – it was giving only trouble: pregnancy.

For centuries women have lived just like factories, reproducing children. Man has used them as factories, not as human beings – because nine children out of ten used to die; so if you want two or three children, the woman has to produce two or three dozen children. That means that for her whole sexual life, while she is capable of giving birth to life, she becomes pregnant, again and again; and pregnancy is a suffering.

She has never been in favor of sex. She has suffered it, she has tolerated it. She has gone into it because it was her duty; and deep down she has hated her husband because he is just like an animal. Why do you think women have always worshipped celibate saints? The innermost reason is that their celibacy proved them to be holier beings.

She cannot respect her own husband in the same way. Once you have a sexual relationship with a woman, she cannot have respect for you. That has been the cost – because she knows you have used her. In every language, the expression makes it clear: it is the man who makes love to the woman, not vice versa. It is strange... they both are making love with each other, but in every language it is always the man who makes love; the woman is only an object. The woman only tolerates and goes into it because she has been conditioned in her mind that it is her duty; the husband is the god, and she has to make his life as pleasant as possible.

But sex has not given anything to her. And she has been kept unaware... because man must have become aware very early, when there was no marriage and when men and women were as free as birds, man must have become aware – and the ancient most women also –

that she has a capacity for multiple orgasm. It is a very dangerous signal to the husband to trigger her orgasmic energies. The husband cannot satisfy her – no husband can satisfy a woman. It seems to be a disparity, a fault of nature, that she can have multiple orgasms and man can have only one orgasm.

So man has tried to avoid even the knowledge that the woman can have orgasm. That's why in the East it is still the case, particularly in the interior parts of the country. Leave aside the modern cities, where a few women may have found out through their education, may have heard the names of Masters and Johnson – who have discovered women's capacity for multiple orgasm.

But in the West it became a problem, because the discovery of multiple orgasm and the centuries old deception by man or woman was a simultaneous growth. At the same time, the women's liberation movement was coming up, and women were trying to find out all the wrongs that had been done to them by men. They suddenly got hold of this new phenomenon, this research, and the most fanatic women's liberation women have become lesbians; because only a woman can help another woman to have multiple orgasm – because it is not concerned with the vagina at all.

Men and women's bodies are very similar, except that the man has only marks of the breasts and the woman has actual breasts; but the man has the marks on his physiology. The clitoris is just a mark of the man's penis; it is just a small growth, but it is outside the vagina. Children are born out of the vagina, and man need not touch the clitoris – and without playing with the clitoris the woman cannot have an orgasm; so it was very simple to avoid it.

The Eastern woman looks more contented because she is not aware of what she is missing. She is more graceful because she has not even started thinking of any liberation. The East, as a whole, has lived under the conditioning of contentment – man and woman both – in poverty, in slavery, in sickness, in death.

The idea of revolution was impossible in the Eastern mind because the conditioning was so strong, and so many centuries old, that whatever you are is the by product of your own actions in past lives. It has nothing to do with the social structure, it has nothing to do with education, it has nothing to do with the division of classes in society, it has nothing to do with men's enslavement of women. The conditioning is so old that one is born with it, and the atmosphere all around is supportive of the conditioning.

All the religions of the East preach that the woman is born a woman because of her past actions; man is a higher being, and the woman is a lower being. This has been accepted. If you are poor, it is not because of exploitation by the rich; you are poor because of your wrong actions in the past.

Man's mind has been diverted from the realities to fictitious explanations – you cannot do anything to change your past life, you have to go through it. Unbelievable religious sects grew in the East – which no reasonable person can accept – but millions followed them. For example, Jainas believe that a woman cannot attain to enlightenment from a woman's body, because she cannot be really celibate. She cannot stop her menstrual period, and that keeps her a sexual being. So unless she attains by being contented, graceful, prayerful, serving her husband and accepting everything as her fate... this is the only way she will be able to be born as a man in the next life.

So nothing can be done right now; right now, one has to simply accept and remain contented. Any rebelliousness will spoil the chances even for the future; any discontentment, any frustration will not only destroy your present, it will destroy your future, too. So the better course, the intelligent course, is to be silent. Nobody can help you, because you did wrong things in your past life – although your poverty is not concerned with your past life.... But that is a very recent finding, and it has not penetrated into the Eastern mind yet.

And just as women have their monthly period, men also have one; that is the very latest finding. So, if her monthly period prevents a woman from being enlightened, it will prevent a man also; just the expression of it is subtle. The woman's expression is physical – you can see the blood every month. But if every man keeps a diary he will be surprised: every month, after twenty eight days, for four or five days he becomes bad-tempered, exactly the way the woman becomes irritable, annoyed at small things.

The same person would not have been annoyed by the same things at another time, but within those four or five days... his period is more psychological, and the woman's period is more physiological; that's the only difference. And it is good for every couple to know perfectly well that when a woman is having her period the man has to be more understanding, that it is beyond her. She will be irritable, she will be easily annoyed, she will become angry, will be more nagging.

In the East, to avoid this, they have found a very strange strategy: during the time of her period, the woman has to live in a dark cell in the house. She has not to come out, she has not to contact anybody – because even her shadow contaminates everything. She cannot prepare the food, and she has to remain aloof and hidden, ashamed of herself. In a way it was good that she rested for those four or five days, did not come in contact with anyone and did not create any unnecessary conflict. But this was one-sided, and unjustified – man also has his period.

The worst combination is when the husband and wife both have their periods together. Then the situation is on the scale of war. But mostly it does not happen – the husband has his period at one time, the wife at a different time. But if the husband keeps a diary for four or five months – just to find which are the dates when his period begins and which are the dates when his period ends – he can allow the wife and the family to know that, for these five days, they have to be a little more tolerant and more compassionate towards him, because he will be in the same situations.

Men and women are not different species. They may differ, but they belong to the same species. Stop that old nonsense – that the woman cannot become enlightened from her body because she cannot prevent her periods; and that it is the obvious proof that she cannot be celibate. Man can only pretend to be celibate because his period is psychological, he has no visible symptoms.

There has been a sect in India, Terapanth. It says that, even if you are passing by the side of a well, and somebody has fallen into the well and is crying, shouting, "Save me! Help me!" just go on your way as if you have not heard him at all – because he is suffering a punishment for some wrong action done in his past life. If you interfere, he will again have to fall into a well. Why give him unnecessary trouble? You are thinking you are helping – you are simply postponing. It is better for him to be finished with the punishment rather than to take your help, come out of the well, and then have to fall in again. He will have to fall in again.

This is one side of the danger – that you have interfered, unnecessarily, because nobody can change his fate, nobody can undo his past, he has to go through all the consequences. Secondly, your interference creates bad consequences for you. You saved the man and he commits a murder tomorrow... then you may not be caught by the police and the courts, but the law of karma – which all Eastern religions believe in – will not forgive you. You have to share the consequences, because if you had not saved him, he could not have murdered. You are a partner – unknowingly, unconsciously, but that does not change the law. The law has to be fulfilled in every condition.

This is the logical end of the theory of the law of karma – the law of action and its consequences. That's why in the East there has been no revolution. And the question of why women look so graceful, and not as frustrated as in the West, is very simple to understand: they have accepted their fate. The Western woman, for the first time in history, is revolting against all these fictitious ideas about fate, the law of karma, past lives.

It is such a nonsense idea – that you did something in your past life, and existence will wait such a long time to punish you. Who is going to keep the records for so many millions of people? And we know it in life – you put your hand... that's what I said to one Jaina monk who was arguing with me about the law of karma. I told him, "There is no problem. You put your hand in the fire, and let us sec whether it burns now or in your next life."

Consequences follow the action immediately. I told him, "Put your hand in..." and he hesitated. I said, "Why are you hesitating? It is a long time... in the next life you will be burned."

He said, "This is a strange way of arguing. You will burn my hand right now."

I said, "That makes you realize that in nature, in life, the action is followed by the consequence, just like you are followed by your shadow. There is not such a gap – you passed by in a past life and in this life we see your shadow passing by – that we simply see your shadow, and we know that somebody must have passed by here in a past life. The consequence is the shadow."

But Western woman has had to pass through a very revolutionary period, which destroyed her contentment – the grace that had always been hers. And it has led her to the extreme; she has started behaving in an ugly and nasty way. It is not a rebelliousness with understanding, it is just a reactionary attitude.

Of the causes that marked the change between the Western woman and the Eastern, the first is Karl Marx. He proposed, and convinced the intelligentsia of the whole world, that poverty has nothing to do with any past life, or with fate, or with destiny; that it is not decided by God, who should be poor and who should be rich. It is the social structure, the economic structure which decides who is going to be poor; and this structure can be changed, because it is not God-made – there is no God, as such – it is man-made.

The Russian revolution proved Karl Marx right, on an experimental basis – that the structure can be changed, that kings can become paupers, and paupers can become kings. And no interference was made by God: You cannot do this, it is my writing on their foreheads, you cannot change it.

The Tsar's whole family in Russia – nineteen people: men and women, old, young, children, one small baby only six months old, and one man ninety-five years old – the whole royal family of nineteen people was massacred. They were cut into pieces, and God did not interfere, saying: "What are you doing with this family?" That is my decision. What are you doing with the people who I have made the owners of almost one-sixth of the world?" The Russian Empire was the biggest empire of those days, and the Tsar was the richest man in the world.

So the first hammering came from Karl Marx. The second hammering came from Sigmund Freud. He declared that men and women are equal, belong to the same species, and any theories or philosophies which condemn women are simply inhuman and male chauvinistic. And then the third, and the last hammering came from Masters and Johnson's researches, which brought to light that the woman has been deprived of orgasm for centuries. It proved that man has been really inhuman in his behavior. As far as his own sexual needs were concerned, he used the woman, but he did not allow the woman to enjoy sex.

These three things have changed the whole atmosphere in the West; but these three things have not yet penetrated into the Eastern, traditional mind. As a result, the Western woman is on the warpath. But it is a reactionary phenomenon; hence I am not in favor of what goes on in the name of women's liberation.

I want women to be liberated, but not to go to the other extreme. The women's liberation movement is going to the other extreme – it is trying to be revengeful; it is trying to do to man exactly what man has done to her. This is sheer stupidity. Past is past: it is no longer there; and what man has done has been done unconsciously. It was not a conscious conspiracy against women. Neither he was aware, nor the woman was aware.

The women's liberation movement is declaring that they don't want to have any relationship with men – cut off all relationships with men. They are promoting lesbianism, a parallel of homosexuality – that women should love only other women and boycott men this is sheer perversion. And as a reaction, women should do everything to man that he has done to her: misbehave, mistreat, use dirty wards as man has always done, smoke cigarettes as man has always done.

Naturally, they are losing their grace, their beauty... dress just as man has always dressed. But it is a strange phenomenon that the way you dress changes so much. The Eastern woman's dress has a grace, and it gives a grace to her whole body. The Western woman is trying to compete with cowboys – blue jeans, stupid-looking clothes, ugly hairdos.

They think, perhaps, they are taking revenge – they are destroying themselves. But revenge always destroys you, reaction always destroys you. I would love to see them as rebels. A rebel knows that to err is human, and to forgive is more human.

The past was full of mistakes of all kinds. Discontinue the past, start everything – man and woman's relationship included – under the light of fresh findings. Find out ways, together, how life can be a beautiful experience, a loving dance without all the ugliness that has happened in the past. Don't repeat it again. It is simply the movement of the pendulum: man was doing idiotic things, now woman will do the idiotic things.

But humanity as a whole goes on suffering. Who does the stupid thing does not matter, but humanity does not evolve. Man and woman have to come to an understanding. They have to forgive the past, and forget it. And they have to start anew with the new findings, remembering one thing – that the woman should not imitate man, because her attraction, her beauty, has a different dimension.

If she imitates man, she will become only a carbon copy of man, she will lose her identity – and she is losing it. The body, in a subtle way, follows your mind.

The Western woman's body is losing the old grace, the old contours. The Western woman does not have such beautiful breasts as she used to have.

What happened? The body follows the mind; she used to have a beautiful curvature, now she is becoming a straight line. And a woman without breasts, a straight line, no curves anywhere, is an ugly phenomenon – it will be such a disgrace. But her clothes will affect her body, her mental attitudes will affect her body. She has not to become a carbon copy of man. She has to become perfect as a woman, and create as much difference between man and herself as possible. The bigger the difference, the more the attraction, the more the beauty, the more the grace. She has to find her own identity.

I am absolutely in favor of liberation – liberation for both man and woman – because it is a simple law: the enslaver also becomes a slave of his own slaves.

Man has enslaved woman, but he has also become a slave. That's why you cannot find a husband who is not really henpecked – at least, I have not found one yet. I have been searching for a husband who is not henpecked. Outside they are all lions – at least members of the Lion's Club. In the house they are not more than rats. And if they had any understanding, they would make a rat's club. That would be true – a henpecked husband's Club.

You cannot enslave anybody without becoming a slave. What you give to others, you have to get back. Give love, and you will get love. Give slavery, and you will get slavery. Whatever you give comes back to you in some form or other. Man and woman both need liberation – liberation from the past, liberation from all the mistakes, all the ugly ideas of the past. And they have to create a new world, a new man, a new woman.

But nothing like this is happening anywhere. I would like my people – particularly the women – to create an authentic women's liberation front, which will not be reactionary, which will not be out of anger and hatred; which will be out of understanding, compassion, love and meditation. Then the Western woman will not lose her grace, will not lose her contentment.

In fact, man also can be more graceful if he allows the woman to be more graceful. Man can also be more beautiful if he allows the woman to be more beautiful. But this means creating more distance – the farther away they are, the more the magnetic pull, the more the attraction, the more the adventure. To see a woman smoking cigarettes – I simply cannot believe my eyes! What else is she going to do next? She will start pissing standing! She has to do everything that man has been doing – all foolishnesses.

The woman has to keep above reactions, and create such a grace and beauty around herself that man will also have to create a more beautiful individuality, a more graceful character. And their meeting should not be anymore in marriage; their meeting should be only of friends – a friendliness, not even friendship. That word "friendship" reminds one of relationship. That "ship" has drowned the whole of humanity. Now no more "ships"; now friendliness, and a deep understanding that nothing is permanent in life.

Even love is a rose flower: in the morning dancing in the wind, in the sun – as if it will remain forever, with such grandeur, with such certainty, with such authority; so fragile and yet so strong against the wind, against the rain, against the sun. But by the evening the petals have withered away, and the rose is gone. That does not mean that it was illusory, it simply means that in life everything is change. And change keeps things new, fresh.

The day marriage disappears, the life of both men and women will become healthier – and certainly longer than you can even imagine. You may not be able to see what the relationship is between long life and marriage. Because marriage is a kind of going against the changing life, it creates a permanent thing; both husband and wife become dull, bored – life loses interest. In fact, they have to destroy their interest, otherwise there is continuous conflict. The husband cannot take an interest in any other woman, the woman cannot laugh with another man. They become prisoners of each other; life becomes a boredom, a routine.

Who wants to live such a life? The will to live becomes weakened. This brings sicknesses, diseases – because their resistance against death is not there. In fact, they start thinking how to finish this whole vicious circle sooner; they start asking deep down in their hearts for death. A will to death arises.

Sigmund Freud was the first man to discover that there is, in the unconscious of man, a will to death. But I have my disagreements with Sigmund Freud. This will to death is not a natural phenomenon – it is a by product of marriage, it is a by product of a bored life. When one starts feeling that living is no longer an adventure, there are no new spaces, no new pastures, then why go on unnecessarily living? Then an eternal sleep in a grave seems to be far more comfortable, far more luxurious, far more joyous.

In no animal does the will to death exist. In the wild, no animal commits suicide. But strangely, in a zoo it has been found that animals commit suicide. And if Sigmund Freud had been studying only zoo animals, he would have concluded that there is a will to death, just as there is a will to life. But the zoo animals are not real animals; and a marriage makes everybody a zoo animal – confined, chained in a thousand and one subtle ways. Sigmund Freud had no idea of wild animals, or wild human beings.

I want human beings to have something of the wild in them. That is my rebel.

He is not going to be part of a zoo, he is going to remain natural. And he is not going to go against life, he is going to flow with life. If man and woman can come to an understanding – which is not difficult at all, which is the simplest thing to do – that we drop being zoo animals, we can gain liberation from the zoo. That's what is needed – liberation from marriage.

And if the woman grows in her natural wildness, and the man grows in his natural wildness, and as strangers they meet in friendliness, their love will have a tremendous depth, a great joy, a blissful dance.

There is no contract, there is no law – love is a law unto itself. And when it disappears, they will say good bye with gratefulness to each other for all those beautiful moments that they have lived together, for all those songs that they have sung together, for all those dances under the full moon, for all those musical moments on the sea beach. They will carry all those golden memories with them, and they will be grateful forever. But they will not hinder each other's freedom; their love prohibits it. Their love should give more freedom. In the past it has been giving more slavery.

There is a tremendous need for the women in the West to start a fresh liberation movement, because the leaders of the present day liberation movement are not meditators, are not sane. They are insane women, fighting against insane men. What is needed is some sanity. What is needed is a deep compassion, even for those who have harmed you in the past out of their unconsciousness – it was not intentional.

But now the women's liberation movement is intentionally trying to harm men – that is even more ugly. It has not gone far, and there are not many women in agreement with these reactionaries. A fresh women's liberation movement can take hold of millions of women who are intelligent and understanding. And this movement will have all the help from men, because then you are not fighting against men, you are fighting against the past – in which you have suffered, in which man has suffered, in which everybody has suffered.

The rebellion is not against man as such, the rebellion is against the past of man and woman both. And then this rebellion will have a quality of religiousness, which will bring grace to people, gratefulness to people. Prem Salila, I hope it is clear to you why the difference in the

Western and the Eastern woman has arisen. It was not there before this century.

I have heard... President Ronald Reagan was gazing down into the center of a famous Greek volcano. Finally he commented: "It looks like hell."

"Ah, you Americans," said the guide. "You have been everywhere."

The Western woman has become more knowledgeable, she has been everywhere. She has become aware of things which the Eastern woman is absolutely innocent of. In her innocence there is a grace, there is a beauty which is not of this world, which gives you some indications of the beyond. That should be the case with every woman in the world.

Every woman can become an arrow towards godliness – her grace, her beauty, her love, her devotion can show you the way towards higher realms of being, greater spaces of consciousness.

A woman is not only capable of giving birth to children, she is also capable of giving birth to seekers of truth. But that side of the woman has not been explored at all. I would like my rebellious people to explore that side too.

The Rebel, (Session 29).

CHAPTER 2

The Fear of Intimacy

I feel so imprisoned by the fear of being intimate and totally losing control with a man. This outrageous woman is locked up inside. When she comes out once in a while, men usually freak out, so she goes back into hibernation, plays safe, and is totally frustrated. Could You please talk about this fear of intimacy?

Mankind, especially womankind, suffers from many sicknesses. Upto now all the so-called civilizations and cultures have been psychologically sick. They have never dared even to recognize their sickness; and the first step of treatment is to recognize that you are sick. The relationship between man and woman has been especially unnatural.

A few facts have to be remembered. Firstly, man has the capacity for only one orgasm; woman has the capacity for multiple orgasms. This has created a tremendous problem. There would not have been any problem if marriage and monogamy had not been imposed on them; it seems it was not the intention of nature. The man becomes afraid of the woman for the simple reason that if he triggers one orgasm in her then she is ready for at least half a dozen more orgasms – and he is incapable of satisfying her.

Secondly, man's sex is local, genital. The same is not the case with woman. Her sexuality, her sensuality is spread all over her body. It takes a longer time for her to warm up, and before she even gets warmed up, the man is finished. He turns his back towards her and starts snoring. For thousands of years, millions of women around the world have lived and died without knowing the greatest natural gift – of orgasmic joy. It was a protection for man's ego. The woman needs a long foreplay so that her whole body starts tingling with sensuality, but then there is the danger: what to do with her capacity for multiple orgasm?

Looked at scientifically, either sex should not be taken so seriously and friends should be invited to give the woman her whole range of orgasms, or some scientific vibrator should be used. But with both there are problems. If you use scientific vibrators, they can give as many orgasms as the woman is capable of; but once a woman has known... then the man's organ looks so poor that she may choose a scientific instrument, a vibrator, rather than a boyfriend. If you allow a few friends to join you, then it becomes a social scandal – that you are indulging in orgies.

So the simplest way man has found is that the woman should not even move while he is making love to her; she should remain almost like a corpse. And man's ejaculation is quick – two minutes, three minutes at the most; by that time the woman is not at all aware of what she has missed.

As far as biological reproduction is concerned, orgasm is not a necessity. But as far as spiritual growth is concerned, orgasm is a necessity.

I have been asked again and again why very few women became enlightened. Amongst other reasons, the most important reason is: they never had any taste of orgasm. The window to the vast sky never opened. They lived, they produced children, and they died. They were used by biology and man, just like factories, producing children.

In the East, even now, it is very difficult to find a woman who knows what orgasm is. I have asked very intelligent, educated, cultured women – they don't have any idea of it. In fact, in the Eastern languages there is no word which can be used as a translation for "orgasm." It was not needed; it was simply never touched.

And man has taught woman that it is only prostitutes who enjoy sex. They moan and they groan and they scream, and they go almost crazy; to be a respectable lady you should not do such things. So the woman remains tense, and feels humiliated deep down – that she has been used. And many women have reported to me that after making love, when their husband goes on snoring, they have wept.

A woman is almost like a musical instrument; her whole body has immense sensitivity, and that sensitivity should be aroused. So there is a need for foreplay. And after making love, the man should not go to sleep; that is ugly, uncivilized, uncultured. A woman who has given you such joy needs some after play too – just out of gratitude.

Your question is very important, and is going to become more and more important in the future. This problem has to be solved; but marriage is a barrier, religion is a barrier, your rotten old ideas are barriers. They are preventing half of humanity from being joyous and their whole energy – that should have blossomed in flowers of joy – turns sour, poisonous, in nagging, in being bitchy; otherwise all this nagging and this bitchiness would disappear.

Men and women should not be in a contract, like marriage. They should be in love – but they should retain their freedom. They don't owe anything to each other.

And life should be more mobile. A woman coming into contact with many friends, a man coming into contact with many women, should be simply the rule. But it is possible only if sex is taken as playfulness, as fun. It is not sin, it is fun. And since the introduction of the pill, now there is no fear about having children. All the implications of the pill have not yet been made available to man. In the past it was difficult, because making love meant more and more children. That was destroying the woman, she was always pregnant; and to remain pregnant and give birth to twelve or twenty children is a tortuous experience.

But the future can be totally different – and the difference will come not from man. Just as Marx said about the proletariat, "Proletariat of the world unite, you have nothing to lose and everything to gain...." He had seen society divided into two classes, the rich and the poor.

I see society divided into two classes: man and woman.

Man has remained the master for centuries, and woman the slave. She has been auctioned, she has been sold, she has been burnt alive. Everything inhuman that can be done has been done to women.

The only way to change the status of women seems to be to allow science full freedom to transform the relationship between man and woman and to drop the idea of marriage, which is absolutely ugly because it is simply a kind of private ownership. Human beings cannot be owned, they are not property. And love should be just a joyful play. And if you want children, then children should belong to the society so the woman is not labeled as mother, as wife, or as prostitute. These labels should be removed.

You are asking, "I feel so imprisoned by the fear of being intimate and totally losing control." Every woman is afraid, because if she loses control with a man, the man freaks out. He cannot handle it; his sexuality is very small. Because he is a donor, he loses energy while making love. The woman does not lose energy while making love – on the contrary, she feels nourished.

Now these are facts which have to be taken into account. Man has for centuries forced the woman to control herself and has kept her at a distance, never allowing her to be too intimate. All his talk about love is bullshit.

"This outrageous woman is locked up inside. When she comes out once in a while, men usually freak out, so she goes back into hibernation, plays safe, and is totally frustrated." This is not only your story, it is the story of all women. They are all living in deep frustration. Finding no way out, knowing nothing about what has been taken away from them, they have only one opening: they will be found in churches, in temples, in synagogues, praying to God. But that God is also a male chauvinist. In the Christian trinity there is no place for a woman. All are men: the father, the son, the holy ghost. It is a gay men's club.

I am reminded that when God first created the world He created man and woman from the mud, and then breathed life into them. He created them equal. But looking at the world, you can understand – whoever has created it is a little stupid. He created man and woman, and made a small bed for them to sleep in. The bed was so small that only one person could sleep on it. They were equal, but the woman insisted: she would be on the bed – he should sleep on the floor. And the problem was the same with the man – he was not willing to sleep on the floor. You will be surprised to know that the first night in existence was the beginning of pillow fights.

They had to go to God. And the solution was very simple – just make a king-size bed; any carpenter could have done it. But God is a man, and is as prejudiced as any other man: He demolished the woman, destroyed her. And then He created Eve, but now woman was no longer equal to man – she was created from one of Adam's ribs; so she was just to serve man, to take care of man, to be used by man.

Christians don't tell you the whole story. They start their story from Adam and Eve – but Eve is already reduced to a state of slavery. And since that day woman has lived in slavery in thousands of ways. Financially she has not been allowed to be independent. Educationally she has not been allowed to be equal to man – because then she could be financially independent. Religiously she has not been allowed even to read the scriptures or listen to somebody else reading the scriptures.

Woman's wings have been cut in many ways.

And the greatest harm that has been done to her is marriage, because neither man nor woman is monogamous; psychologically they are polygamous. So their whole psychology has been forced against its own nature. And because woman was dependent on man she had to suffer all kinds of insults – because man was the master, he was the owner, he had all the money.

To satisfy his polygamous nature, man created prostitutes. Prostitutes are a by-product of marriage.

And this ugly institution of prostitution will not disappear from the world unless marriage disappears. It is its shadow – because man does not want to be tied to a monogamous relationship, and he has the freedom of movement, he has the money, he has the education, he has all the power. He invented prostitutes; and to destroy a woman by making her a prostitute is the ugliest murder you can do.

The strange fact is, all religions are against prostitution – and they are the cause of it. They are all for marriage, and they cannot see a simple fact, that prostitution came into existence with marriage.

Now the women's liberation movement is trying to imitate all the stupidities that men have done to women. In London, in New York, in San Francisco, you can find male prostitutes. That is a new phenomenon. This is not a revolutionary step, this is a reactionary step.

The problem is that unless you lose control while making love, you will not have an orgasmic experience. So at least my people should be more understanding, that the woman will moan and groan and scream. It is because her whole body is involved – total involvement. You need not be afraid of that. It is tremendously healing: she will not be bitchy towards you, and she will not nag you, because all the energy that becomes bitchiness has been transformed into an immense joy. And don't be afraid about the neighbors – it is their problem if they are worried about your groaning and moaning, it is not your problem. You are not preventing them....

Make your love a really festive affair, don't make it a hit-and-run affair. Dance, sing, play music – and don't let sex be cerebral. Cerebral sex is not authentic; sex should be spontaneous.

Create the situation. Your bedroom should be a place as holy as a temple. In your bedroom don't do anything else; sing and dance and play, and if love happens on its own, as a spontaneous thing, you will be immensely surprised that biology has given you a glimpse of meditation.

And don't be worried about the woman who is going crazy. She has to go crazy – her whole body is in a totally different space. She cannot remain in control; if she controls it she will remain like a corpse.

Millions of people are making love to corpses.

I have heard a story about Cleopatra, the most beautiful woman. When she died, according to the old Egyptian rituals her body was not buried for three days. She was raped in those three days – a dead body. When I first came to know about it, I was surprised: what kind of man would have raped her? But then I felt perhaps it was not so strange a fact. All men have reduced women to corpses, at least while they are making love.

When the Christian missionaries came to the East, they were surprised to realize that they knew only one posture: man on top – because then man has more mobility, and the woman is lying like a corpse underneath him.

The man on top is very uncultured; the woman is more fragile. But why men have chosen to be on the top is so that they can keep the woman under control. Crushed under the beast, beauty is bound to be under control. The woman is not even to open her eyes, because that is like a prostitute. She has to behave like a lady. This posture, man on top, is known in the East as the missionary posture.

A great revolution is ahead in the relationship between man and woman. There are institutes evolving around the world, in the advanced countries, where they teach you how to love. It is unfortunate that even animals know how to love, and man has to be taught. And in their teaching, the basic thing is foreplay and after play. Then love becomes such a sacred experience.

You should drop the fear of being intimate and totally losing control with a man. Let the idiot be afraid; if he wants to be afraid, that is his business. You should be authentic and true to yourself. You are lying to yourself, you are deceiving yourself, you are destroying yourself.

What is the harm if the man freaks out and runs out of the room naked? Close the door! Let the whole neighborhood know that this man is mad. But you need not control your possibility of having an orgasmic experience. The orgasmic experience is the experience of merging and melting, egolessness, mindlessness, timelessness.

This may trigger your search for finding a way

that, without any man, without any partner, you can drop the mind, you can drop time, and you can enter into orgasmic joy on your own. I call this authentic meditation.

Don't be worried, enjoy the whole game – be playful about it. If one man freaks out, there are millions of other men. You will find some mad guy one day who does not freak out!

The Razor's Edge, (Session 26).

CHAPTER 3

Man's Conspiracy

Why is it so difficult for me to see the worth of my feminine qualities? There is still something in me that judges them as weak and having a feeling of not being able to survive.

It is the long condemnation of feminine qualities that has gone deep into the blood and bones of women. It is man's conspiracy to prove himself superior to woman – which he is not.

Man is deep down aware of the fact that the woman has something which he does not have. In the first place the woman is attractive to him, she looks beautiful. He falls in love with the woman, the woman becomes almost an addiction to him – and that is where the trouble arises.

The feeling of dependence on woman, which every man feels, makes him react in such a way that he tries to manage the woman as a slave – spiritually a slave. He's also afraid because she is beautiful... she is beautiful not only to him, but to whomever comes in contact with her. Great jealousy arises in the egoist, male chauvinist mind.

He has done with women what Machiavelli suggests to the politicians – marriage is politics too. Machiavelli suggests that the best way of defence is offence, and man has used the idea for centuries – centuries before Machiavelli recognized it as a basic fact in all political spheres. Wherever there is some kind of domination, offence is certainly the best way of defence. In defence, you are already losing ground; you have already accepted yourself as the defeated side. You are just protecting yourself.

In India hundreds of invaders have come – small groups of invaders, but they conquered this vast country, which is a subcontinent; it is a world in itself. By the end of this century, one man in every four will be Indian. It is one-fourth of humanity.

In this country there are religious scriptures like Manusmriti, five thousand years old, and they suggest that if you want to have peace in your house, giving a good beating to the woman once in a while is absolutely necessary. She should be kept almost imprisoned. And that's how she has lived – in different cultures, different countries, but her imprisonment has been almost the same. And because man wanted to prove himself superior.... Remember, whenever you want to prove something, that means you are not that thing.

A real superiority needs no proof, no evidence, no witness, no argument. A real superiority is immediately recognized by anybody who has even a small amount of intelligence. The real superiority has its own magnetic force.

Because men condemned woman – and they had to condemn her to keep her under control – they reduced her almost to a subhuman category. What fear must have reduced man to do this? – because it is sheer paranoia.... Man continuously compares and finds the woman superior. For example, in making love to a woman a man is very inferior because he can have only one orgasm at a time, while the woman can have at least half a dozen, a chain – multiple orgasm. Man simply feels utterly helpless: he cannot give those orgasms to the woman.

This has created one of the most miserable things in the world: because he cannot give her a multiple orgasm he has tried not to give her even the first orgasm. The taste of the orgasm can create danger for him. If the woman knows what orgasm is she is bound to become aware that one orgasm is not satisfying; on the contrary, she is more thirsty. But the man is spent. So the most cunning way is not to let the woman know that anything like orgasm exists in the world.

It is only in this century that we have given recognition to a certain orgasmic state while making love. No sex manual, no treatise written on sex in the East or the West even mentions the word "orgasm." It seems to be a conspiracy. Vatsyayana – the first man in the history to write about sex energy, to explore it in a scientific way – wrote the first treatise on sexology five thousand years ago: Kamasutras, aphorisms on sex.

He has gone into the subject as deeply as possible from all directions; he has not ignored the smallest detail. He describes eighty-four postures of love making. You cannot improve on it, you cannot find an eighty-fifth posture; he has done exhaustive work. But even Vatsyayana does not mention orgasm. That is simply unbelievable – that a man who enquired so deeply into sex did not come across the fact of orgasm.

No, my feeling is that he is hiding a fact – and to hide any fact is a crime, because that means you allow the false to continue as if it is the truth. And it is not an ordinary fact concerning chemistry or geography; it is something which is the most important in human life.

The experience of orgasm not only gives you the ultimate pleasure the body is capable of, it also gives you the insight that this is not all. It opens a door. It makes you aware that you have been unnecessarily looking outside; your real treasure is within.

Meditation has been found by people who had deep orgasmic experiences. Meditation is a by product of orgasmic experience. There is no other way to find meditation. But orgasm brings you naturally into a state of meditation: time stops, thinking disappears, the ego is no more. You are pure energy. For the first time you understand you are not the body and you are not the mind; you are something that transcends both – a conscious energy.

And once you enter into the realm of conscious energy, you start having the most beautiful experiences of life, the lightest, the most colorful, the most poetic, the most creative. They give you fulfillment and contentment on the one hand – as far as the body, the mind and the world are concerned. On the other hand, they create a tremendous, divine discontentment, because what you have experienced is great, but the very experience of it makes you certain, for no reason at all, that there must be greater experiences ahead.

Before you knew anything about orgasm, you had never dreamed about it; now you know it. This is going to become an incentive to seek and search: Is there anything more juicy, more blissful, more psychedelic than any psychedelics can deliver to you?

This search led man toward meditation.

It was a simple insight into the orgasmic experience.

What happens? Time stops, thinking disappears. The feeling of "I" is no more there. There is a feeling of "isness" – pure, existential – but there is no ego attached to it. I, me, mine – they have all been left far behind. This gives you the clue for meditation. If you can manage a transcendence of time, a transcendence of mind, you will be entering into orgasmic space alone – without a woman, without a man. To be exactly true, meditation is non-sexual orgasm.

But half of humanity has not known orgasm for centuries. And because the woman has not known orgasm, you should not think that man has been in a better position. Not giving orgasm to the woman he has to lose his own orgasm too. (...) So the woman has lost something tremendously beautiful, something sacred on the earth – and the man has lost something too.

Orgasm is not the only thing in which the woman is powerful. Everywhere in the world the woman lives five years longer than the man; her average age is five years more than the man's. That means she has more resistance, more stamina. Women are sick less than men. Women, even if they are sick, heal themselves more quickly than men. These are scientific facts.

One hundred and fifteen boys are born while one hundred girls are born. One wonders: why one hundred and fifteen? But nature knows better. By the time they are marriageable, fifteen boys will have popped off! Only one hundred boys and one hundred girls will be left. Girls don't die easily.

Women go mad less than men. Again, the proportion is the same: men go mad twice as often as women.

And still, after all these facts established by science, the superstition continues that man is stronger. Only in one thing is he stronger, and that is that he has a muscular body; he is a good manual worker. Otherwise, on every point he feels – and he has felt for centuries – a deep inferiority complex.

To avoid that complex, the only way is to force the woman into an inferior position. And that is the only thing that is more powerful in man: he can force the woman. He is more cruel, he is more violent, and he has forced the woman to accept an idea which is absolutely false – that she is weak. And to prove that the woman is weak, he has to condemn all the feminine qualities. He has to say that they are all weak, and all those qualities together make the woman weak.

In fact, the woman has all the great qualities in her. And whenever a man becomes awakened, he attains to the same qualities which he has been condemning in women. The qualities that are thought to be weak are all the feminine qualities. And it is a strange fact that all the great qualities come into that category. What is left are only the brutal qualities, animal qualities.

Strength has many dimensions. Love has its own strength. For example, to carry a child in the womb for nine months needs strength, stamina, love. No man could manage it. An artificial womb could be placed in man – now scientific technology has come to the point where man could have a plastic womb implanted – but I don't think he could survive nine months! They are both going to jump into the ocean.

It is difficult to give life to another soul, to give a

body to another soul, to give a brain and mind to another soul. The woman shares wholeheartedly in giving to the child whatever she can manage. And even after the child is born, it is not easy to bring up children. To me, it seems to be the most difficult thing in the world.

Astronauts and Edmund Hillary... these people should first try to bring up children. Then only can we accept that they have done something by going to Everest; otherwise it is pointless. Even if you have reached the moon and walked on the moon it does not matter: it doesn't show that you are stronger.

A living child – so volatile, such an energy overflowing that he will tire you within hours. Nine months in the womb and then a few years.... Just try one night with a small baby in your bed. During that night, in your house, something is going to happen: either the child will kill you or you will kill the child. Most probably you will kill the child, because children are the nastiest people in the world. They are so fresh and they want to do so many things and you are dead tired. You want to go to sleep, and the child is fully awake: he wants to do all kinds of things and he wants your advice, and questions... and if nothing works then he wants to go to the bathroom! He is feeling thirsty... he is feeling hungry in the middle of the night....

I don't think there is any man who can have a pregnancy or who can bring up children. It is the strength of the woman. But it is a different strength. There is one strength which is destructive, there is another strength which is creative. There is one strength which is of hatred, and there is another strength which is of love.

Love, trust, beauty, sincerity, truthfulness, authenticity – these are all feminine qualities, and they are far greater than any qualities that man has. But the whole past has been dominated by man and his qualities. Naturally in war, love is of no use, truth is of no use, beauty is of no use, aesthetic sensibility is no use. In war you need a heart that is more stony than stones. In war you need simply hate, anger, a madness to destroy.

In three thousand years man has fought five thousand wars. Yes, this is also strength but not worthy of human beings. This is strength derived from our animal inheritance. It belongs to the past, which is gone; and the feminine qualities belong to the future, which is coming.

There is no need to feel yourself weak because of your feminine qualities. You should feel grateful to existence that what man has to earn, you have been given by nature as a gift.

Man has to learn how to love. Man has to learn how to let the heart be the master and the mind be just an obedient servant. Man has to learn these things – the woman brings these things with her. But we condemn all these qualities as weaknesses. Even if you have chosen women as great individuals, you can see what you have chosen – you have chosen a man, because you have chosen the qualities of man that were in the woman.

For example, Joan of Arc had all the qualities of man. The Queen of Jhansi in India had all the qualities of man: she could fight with a naked sword, could kill people without any problem. Such women have been chosen in history and great tribute has been paid to them by the historians. And they don't represent women; in fact that is the reason why they have been chosen – because they are just carbon copies of men.

The women's liberation movement has to learn one fundamental thing: that is, not to imitate men and not to listen to what he says about feminine qualities, the feminine personality. Drop all the ideas of man that he has been putting in your heads. And also drop the ideas of the women's liberation movement, because they are also putting nonsense into your minds. Their nonsense is that they are trying to prove that men and women are equal. They are not – and when I say they are not, I don't mean that someone is superior and someone is inferior. I mean that they are unique.

Women are women and men are men; there is no question of comparison. Equality is out of the question. They are not unequal and neither can they be equal: They are unique.

Rejoice in your feminine qualities, make a poetry of your feminine qualities. That is your great inheritance from nature. Don't throw it away, because the man does not have them.

I would like the whole world to be full of feminine qualities. Then only can wars disappear. Then only can marriage disappear. Then only can nations disappear. Then only can we have one world: a loving, a peaceful, a silent and beautiful world.

So drop all the conditionings man has given to you. Find your own qualities and develop them. You are not to imitate the man; neither is the man to imitate you. There is no need of any conflict between you, because you are man and woman together; simultaneously.

Rather than creating a conflict, my whole work is to indicate to you the path, how you can create an orchestra of all your qualities together. That will be your wholeness as a human being.

Sermons in Stones, Chapter 17.

CHAPTER 4

Your Male Chauvinist Attitude Hurts

I hate women. Why do you
put women on the way of Tao?
Woman is what man made of
her. It is a vicious circle.

Women have as much intelligence as any man – because intelligence has no concern with sexual hormones. Do you think if you changed Albert Einstein into a woman with plastic surgery, he would lose his intelligence? He would still remain Albert Einstein, but in a woman's body. The difference is only of bodies; the difference is not of consciousness, not of intelligence.

But unfortunately man decided to repress woman.

For centuries it has not been clear to historians why it had to happen in such a way. But the latest psychological research makes it very clear why it happened: it happened because man feels a deep inferiority complex in comparison to woman.

And the basic root of that feeling comes from the woman's capacity to become a mother. She is the source of life, she creates life. Man is incapable of it. This became the reason to cut the wings of all women – of freedom, of education – and confine her to a prison-like home and reduce her to just a factory of reproduction so that he can forget that he is inferior.

The woman had to be made inferior so that man could feel at ease, so that his ego could feel that now there is no competition with women at all.

The woman is not the cause of all her bitchiness: You have been torturing her for thousands of years. No society in the world has accepted her as equal to man.

No culture of the past has given the woman the same respect as it gives to the man; on the contrary, they have all tried to force her into a subhuman existence.

And the reason why the woman did not revolt against such things is simple: again, the same motherhood. For nine months when she is pregnant, she becomes absolutely dependent – particularly in a society which lived by hunting. And by the way, I would like you to remember that the society in which you are living now – where houses exist, cities exist – is a contribution of women, not of men. The house is the woman's contribution.

Man was hunting. The woman was confined to a small space; naturally she started decorating it, cleaning it, making it beautiful, liveable – and she became attached. In a hunting society, the nomads had to go on changing… because when hunting was not giving them enough food they had to move to where the animals were. They could not have permanent cities; they could have only tents, not houses.

And you can see it: when a man lives alone, his house is almost like a tent, it is not like a house. Without a woman it remains a tent, a temporary place – just a shelter with nothing sacred about it. As the woman enters, the tent starts transforming into a house and finally into a home.

In hunting societies the woman's function was nothing but reproduction; she was continuously pregnant. This became her failure: she could not fight, she could not rebel, she had to submit, she had to surrender – of course unwillingly. Nobody becomes a slave willingly.

When somebody becomes a slave willingly, there is no problem. But millions of women have been forced to become slaves unwillingly. Naturally they try to take revenge in indirect ways.

Your male chauvinist attitude hurts.

It is simply an unconscious reaction, and you have to be watchful of the reaction so that it can disappear. It is undignified of you. It shows something about you – not about the woman. It is your anger, it is your hate. If you will look at the history....

In many villages the women cannot enter the temples. In some religions she can enter, but she has a separate section – not the same as the men. In all religions the woman is not accepted as a candidate for the ultimate growth of consciousness. She is unworthy, not for any other reason – just because she is a woman; her crime is that she is a woman. And she can evolve but she will have to fulfill a condition: first she will have to be born as a man.

These are subtle ways of humiliation, of cutting women off from the world of power, from the world where everything is happening. The woman is not part of it. She is not part of your wars, she is not part of your businesses, she is not part of your religions. The society is made by men. Women are living in a society which is not made for them, not made by them; it has not considered them at all.

Your anger towards women is worth understanding. Perhaps it is really your anger against yourself, your anger against men – what men have done to women.

Women have been victims. You cannot be angry with them. In the home, the husband is the victim; and it can be said without any doubt that every husband is henpecked. In fact, every intelligent husband has to be – only some idiot may not be. But this is the price that every man has to pay for what mankind has been doing to womankind for thousands of years.

If you want to get free from your anger against women, you will have to go through a very deep inner spring cleaning and see that the woman is the victim. And because she is the victim and has no positive way to resist, to fight, she finds indirect ways: of nagging, of screaming, of throwing tantrums. These are simply hopeless efforts. And naturally her rage against the whole of humanity becomes focused on one man, the husband.

The freedom of women is going to be the freedom of men too. The day the woman is accepted as equal, given equal opportunity to grow, man will find himself suddenly free from the bitchiness that he used to feel from the women. It is time. Man has come to a certain maturity.

We can create a world together, with men and women sharing their insight, their visions, their dreams. Because they are different, their dreams are different, their contributions to the society will be different. And if a society can be created in which men and women have participated equally, that will be for the first time the richest society in the world.

Sermons in Stones, Chapter 5.

CHAPTER 5

Nobody Wants To Be Used

Why do women like to be
attractive to men when they also
resent men's sexual desires?

There is a political strategy in it. Women like to be attractive because that gives power; the more attractive they are, the more powerful they are over men. And who does not want to be powerful? Their whole lives people are struggling to be powerful.

Why do you desire money? – it will bring power. Why do you want to become the prime minister or the president of a country? – it will bring power. Why do you want to become a saint? – it brings power. People are searching for power in different ways. You have not left women any other sources to be powerful – only one outlet: their bodies. That's why they are continuously interested in being more and more attractive.

Have you not watched it, that the modern woman does not care so much about being attractive? Why? – because she is entering into other kinds of power politics. The modern woman is getting out of the old bondage. She will fight the man in the universities for the degrees; she will compete in the marketplace; she will compete in politics. She need not be worried too much about looking very attractive.

Man has never bothered much to look attractive. Why? That has been left completely to women. For women that was the only source to attain some power. And for men there were so many other sources that to look attractive looked a little bit effeminate, sissy. That is for women.

This has not been always so. There was a time in the past when women were as free as men. Then men used to be interested in being attractive as much as women were. Look at Krishna, his picture – with beautiful silk robes, with a flute, with all kinds of ornaments, earrings, with a beautiful crown made of peacock feathers. Look at him! – he looks so beautiful. Those were the days when men and women were absolutely free to do whatsoever they wanted to do. Then came a long, long dark age when women were repressed.

It happened because of the priests and your so-called saints. Your saints have always been afraid of women, because the woman seems to be so powerful that she can destroy the saint's sainthood within minutes. It is because of your saints that women were condemned. They were afraid of women: women have to be repressed. And because women were repressed, all sources of competing in life, flowing in life, were taken away. Then there was only one thing left: their bodies.

And who does not want to be powerful? Unless you understand that power only brings misery, power is destructive, violent; unless through understanding your desire for power disappears – who does not like to be powerful?

The woman remains powerful only when she goes on hanging in front of you like a carrot – never available and always available, so close and so far away. Then only is she powerful. If she immediately falls into your lap, then the power is gone. And once you have exploited her sexuality, once you have used her, she is finished, she has no more power over you. So she attracts you and yet keeps aloof. She attracts you, she provokes you, she seduces you, and when you come close to her, she simply says no!

Now that is simple logic. If she says yes, you reduce her to a mechanism; you use her. And nobody wants to be used. It is the other side of the same power politics. Power means the capacity to use the other, and when somebody uses you your power is gone, you are reduced to powerlessness.

So no woman wants to be used. And you have been doing that down the ages. Love has become an ugly thing. It should be the greatest glory, but it is not – because man has been using woman and the woman resents it, resists it, naturally. She does not want to be reduced to a commodity.

That's why you will see husbands just wagging their tails around their wives, and their wives in such an attitude that they are above all this nonsense – holier-than-thou. The wives go on pretending that they are not interested in sex, ugly sex. They are as interested as you are, but the problem is, they cannot show their interest, otherwise you immediately reduce them to powerlessness, you start using them.

So they are interested in everything else, in being very attractive to you – and then denying you. That is the joy of power: pulling you and you are pulled almost as if pulled by strings – and then saying no to you, reducing you to absolute powerlessness. And you are wagging your tail like a dog – then the woman enjoys.

This is an ugly state. This should not be so. This is an ugly state because love has been reduced to power politics. This has to be changed.

We have to create a new humanity and a new world, in which love will not be a question of power at all. At least take love out of power politics. Leave money, leave politics there – leave everything there, but take love out of it. Love is something immensely valuable; don't make it a thing of the marketplace. But that's what has happened.

The woman tries in every way to be beautiful – at least to look beautiful. And once you are trapped into her allurements, she starts escaping from you, because that is the whole game. If you start escaping from her, she will come close to you, she will start following you. The moment you start following her, she will start escaping. This is the game! This is not love; this is inhuman. But this is what is happening and has been happening down the ages. Beware if it!

At least in my commune this has to disappear. Each person has tremendous dignity, and no person can ever be reduced to a commodity, to a thing. Respect men, respect women – they are all divine.

And forget the old idea that it is the man who makes love to the woman – that is so stupid. It makes it feel as if man is the doer and the woman is just there as something to be done to. Even in the language it is man who makes love, it is man who is the acting partner; it is the woman who is just there, a passive receptivity. This is not true. Both are making love to each other, both are doers, both are participants – the woman in her own way. Receptivity is her way of participating, but it is participation as much as the man's.

And don't think that only you are doing something to the woman: she is also doing something to you. You are both doing something tremendously valuable to each other. You are offering yourselves to each other; you are sharing your energies with each other. You are both offering yourselves in the temple of love, in the temple of the god of love. It is the god of love who has possessed both of you. It is a very sacred moment. You are walking on holy ground. And then there will be a totally different quality in people's behavior.

It is good to be beautiful. It is ugly to appear to be beautiful. It is good to be attractive, but it is ugly to manage to be attractive. That management is cunningness. And people are naturally beautiful, there is no need for any make-up. All make-up is ugly, it makes you more and more ugly. The beauty is in simplicity, in innocence, in being natural, in being spontaneous. And when you are beautiful, don't use that beauty as power politics – that is profaning it, that is sacrilegious.

Beauty is a gift of God. Share, but don't use it in any way for domination, for possessing the other. And your love will become a prayer, and your beauty will become an offering to God.

Philosophia Perennis, Volume II, Chapter 4.

[illegible] but it is [illegible] participation [illegible]

[illegible] means doing something [illegible] doing something [illegible] others [illegible]

[illegible] be beautiful [illegible] good [illegible] really [illegible] but [illegible]

[illegible]

[illegible]

CHAPTER 6

Without Freedom, Love Dies

Is it possible to be married and
to be free at the same time?

It is difficult, but not impossible. Just a little understanding is needed.

A few basic truths have to be recognized. One is that nobody is born for another. The second is that nobody is here to fulfill your ideals of how he should be. The third is that you are master of your own love, and you can give as much as you want – but you cannot demand love from the other person, because nobody is a slave. If these simple facts are understood, then it does not matter whether you are married or unmarried, you can be together – allowing space to each other, never interfering in each other's individuality.

In fact marriage is an out-of-date institution. In the first place, to live in any institution is not good. Any institution is destructive. Marriage has destroyed almost all possibilities of happiness for millions of people – and all for useless things. In the first place, marriage – the very ritual of marriage – is bogus.

If you take marriage non-seriously, then you can be free. If you take it seriously, then freedom is impossible. Take marriage just as a game – it is a game. Have a little sense of humor, that it is a role you are playing on the stage of life; but it is not something that belongs to existence or has any reality – it is a fiction. But people are so stupid that they even start taking fiction for reality.

I have seen people reading fiction with tears in their eyes, because in the fiction things are going so tragically. It is a very good device in the movies that they put the lights off so everybody can enjoy the movie, laugh, cry, be sad, be happy. If there was light it would be a little difficult – what will others think? And they know perfectly well that the screen is empty, there is nobody; it is just a projected picture. But they forget it completely. And the same has happened with our lives. Many things which are simply to be taken humorously, we take so seriously – and from that seriousness begins our problem.

In the first place, why should you get married? You love someone, live with someone – it is part of your basic rights. You can live with someone, you can love someone.

Marriage is not something that happens in heaven; it happens here, through the crafty priests. But if you want to join the game with society and don't want to stand alone and aloof, you make it clear to your wife or to your husband that this marriage is just a game: "Never take it seriously. I will remain as independent as I was before marriage, and you will remain as independent as you were before marriage. Neither I am going to interfere in your life, nor are you going to interfere in my life; we will live as two friends together, sharing our joys, sharing our freedom – but not becoming a burden on each other."

"And any moment we feel that the spring has passed, the honeymoon is over, we will be sincere enough not to go on pretending, but to say to each other that we loved much – and we will remain grateful to each other forever, and the days of love will haunt us in our memories, in our dreams, as golden – but the spring is over. Our paths have come to a point where, although it is sad, we have to part, because now living together is not a sign of love. If I love you, I will leave you the moment I see my love has become a misery to you. If you love me, you will leave me the moment you see that your love is creating an imprisonment for me."

Love is the highest value in life.

It should not be reduced to stupid rituals.

And love and freedom go together – you cannot choose one and leave the other. A man who knows freedom is full of love, and a man who knows love is always willing to give freedom. If you cannot give freedom to the person you love, to whom can you give freedom? Giving freedom is nothing but trusting.

Freedom is an expression of love.

So whether you are married or not, remember, all marriages are fake – just social conveniences. Their purpose is not to imprison you and bind you to each other; their purpose is to help you to grow with each other. But growth needs freedom; and in the past, all the cultures have forgotten that without freedom, love dies.

The Rebellious Spirit, Session 8.

CHAPTER 7

Only A Thing Can Be Possessed

Please speak about
becoming a mother.

To become a mother is one of the greatest responsibilities in the world. So many people are in on the psychiatrist's couches and so many people are in madhouses and so many mad people are out of the madhouses. If you go deep into the neurosis of humanity you will always find the mother, because so many women want to be mothers but they don't know how to be. Once the relationship between the mother and the child goes wrong, the child's whole life goes wrong, because that is his first contact with the world, his first relationship. Everything else will be in continuity with it. And if the first step goes wrong, the whole life goes wrong.

One should become a mother knowingly. You are taking on one of the greatest responsibilities that a human being can take.

Men are a little freer in that way because they cannot take the responsibility of becoming a mother. Women have more responsibility. So become a mother, but don't take it for granted that just by being a woman one is necessarily a mother – that is a fallacy. Motherhood is a great art; you have to learn it. So start learning about it!

A few things I would like to say to you.

First, never treat the child as yours; never possess the child. The child comes through you but it is not yours.

God has only used you as a vehicle, a medium, but the child is not your possession. Love, but never possess the child. If the mother starts possessing the child then the life is destroyed. The child starts becoming a prisoner. You are destroying his personality and you are reducing him to a thing. Only a thing can be possessed: a house can be possessed, a car can be possessed – never a person. So this is the first lesson – get ready for it. Before the child comes you should be able to greet him as an independent being, as a person in his own right, not just your child.

And the second thing: treat the child as you would treat a grown-up person.

Never treat a child like a child. Treat the child with deep respect. God has chosen you to be a host. God has entered into your being as a guest. The child is very fragile, helpless. It is very difficult to respect the child. It is very easy to humiliate the child. Humiliation comes very easy because the child is helpless and cannot do anything, cannot retaliate, cannot react.

Treat the child as a grown-up, and with great respect. Once you respect the child, you don't try to impose your ideas on him. You don't try to impose anything on the child. You simply give him the freedom – freedom to explore the world. You help him to become more and more powerful in exploring the world but you never give him directions. You give him energy, you give him protection, you give him security – all that he needs – but you help him to go farther away from you to explore the world.

And of course in freedom the wrong is also included.

It is very difficult for a mother to learn that when you give freedom to a child it is not freedom only to do good; it is also necessarily the freedom to do bad, to do wrong. So make the child alert, intelligent, but never give him any commandments – nobody keeps them, and people become hypocrites. So if you really love the child, then one thing has to be remembered: never, never help him in any way, force him in any way to become a hypocrite.

And the third thing: don't listen to the morality, don't listen to religion, don't listen to culture – listen to nature. Whatsoever is natural is good – even if sometimes it is very difficult for you, very uncomfortable for you... because you have not been brought up according to nature. Your parents were not bringing you up with real art, love. It was just an accidental thing. Don't repeat the same mistakes. Many times you will feel very uneasy. ...

For example, a small child starts playing with his sexual organs. The natural tendency of the mother is to stop the child because she has been taught that this is wrong. Even if she feels that nothing is wrong, if somebody is there she feels a little embarrassed. Feel embarrassed! That is your problem; that has nothing to do with the child. Feel embarrassed. Even if you lose respectability in society, lose it – but never interfere with the child. Let nature take its own course. You are there to facilitate whatsoever nature is unfolding. You are not to direct nature, you are just to be there as a help.

So these three things... and start meditating. Before

the child is born you should go as deeply as possible in meditation. When the child is within your womb, whatsoever you are doing continuously goes as a vibration to the child. If you are angry, your stomach has a tension of anger. The child immediately feels it. When you are sad, your stomach has an atmosphere of sadness. Immediately the child feels dull, depressed. The child totally depends on you. Whatsoever is your mood is the mood of the child. The child has no independence right now: your climate is his climate. So no more fighting, no more anger. That's why I say that to be a mother is a great responsibility. You will have to sacrifice much.

If from the very beginning anger, hatred, conflict, enters into the child's mind, then you are causing hell for him; he will suffer. Then it is better not to bring a child into the world. Why bring a child into suffering? The world is tremendous suffering.

In the first place bringing a child into this world is a very risky affair. But even if you want that, at least bring a child who will be totally different in this world – who will not be miserable, who will at least help the world to be a little more celebrating. He will bring a little more festivity into the world... a little more laughter, love, life.

God is Not for Sale.

CHAPTER 8

Love Is Like A Bird On The Wing

In my sixty-three years of
life You are the first love
relationship which has made
me independent. How has this
happened?

Love brings freedom. And a love that does not bring freedom is not love.

Love is not domination. How can you dominate someone you love? How can you make him dependent, and still be loving? But that's what goes on happening in the world in the name of love, something else – a lust to power, to dominate the other. Naturally independence cannot be allowed. Every effort is made that the other should be a carbon copy of you. You are afraid of the freedom of the other, because freedom is not controllable, and freedom is not predictable. So all so-called love tries in every way to destroy freedom – and the moment freedom is destroyed, love dies.

Love is very fragile, just like a rose flower. You have to allow it to dance in the rain, in the wind, in the sun.

Love is like a bird on the wing, having the whole sky as its freedom. You can catch hold of the bird, you can put it in a beautiful golden cage, and it seems it is the same bird that was flying in freedom and had the whole sky to itself. It only appears to be the same bird, it is not: you have killed it. You have cut its wings. You have taken away its sky. And the birds don't bother about your gold – however precious may be your cage, it is imprisonment.

And that's what we are doing with our love: we

create golden cages. We are afraid because the sky is vast. The fear is, the bird may not return. To keep it under your control it has to be imprisoned. That's how love becomes marriage. Love is a bird on the wing: marriage is a bird in a golden cage. And certainly the bird can never forgive you. You have destroyed all its beauty, all its joy, all its freedom. You have destroyed its spirit – it is just a dead replica. But you have made one thing certain, that it cannot escape you, that it will be always yours, that tomorrow also it will be yours, and the day after tomorrow....

Lovers are always afraid. The fear is because love comes like a breeze. You cannot produce it, it is not something to be manufactured – it comes. But anything that comes on its own, can go also on its own; that is a natural corollary. Love comes, and flowers blossom in you, songs arise in your heart, a desire to dance... but with a hidden fear. What will happen if this breeze that has come to you – cool and fragrant – leaves you tomorrow?... because you are not the limit of existence. And the breeze is only a guest – it will be with you as long as it feels to be, and it will go any moment.

This creates fear in people, and they become possessive. They start closing their doors and windows to keep the breeze in; but when your doors and windows are closed, it is not the same breeze. The coolness is lost, the fragrance is lost – soon it is disgusting. It needs freedom, and you have taken away the freedom – it is only a corpse.

In the name of love people are carrying each others' corpses – which they call marriage. And to carry corpses you have to go to a government registrar's office to make it a legal bond. Love cannot allow marriage. In an authentic world marriage will be impossible.

One should love, and love intensely and love totally, and not be worried about tomorrow. If existence has been so blissful today, trust that existence will be more beautiful and more blissful tomorrow. As your trust grows, existence becomes more and more generous towards you. More love will shower on you. More flowers of joy and ecstasy will rain over you.

In your sixty-three years' life, whatever you have known in the name of love was not love. It may have been infatuation, it may have been biological attraction, it may have been a conspiracy of hormones against two individuals – but not love. You have known love for the first time... because this is the only criterion: your freedom grows deeper; your independence becomes more solid and integrated and crystallized. This is the only criterion that love has visited you, that love has been a guest in your heart.

And who cares about tomorrow? The people who care about tomorrow are the people who don't have today, who are miserable right now and try to hide it, try to ignore it in the hope, in the desire, in the dream for tomorrow. But tomorrow never comes. This is one of the difficulties: it is always today that comes; and you become accustomed to being miserable today, and hoping, desiring, dreaming for tomorrow. You have missed life. People have become so accustomed to tomorrows that they are not only thinking in this life of tomorrows, they are thinking of life after death.

People used to ask me, "What will happen after life? What will happen after death?" And I used to say to them, "What is happening before death, the same will continue. Are you blissful today? – because tomorrow will be born out of today. Today is pregnant with your whole future."

Love intensely, joyously, totally, and you will never think of creating a bondage, a contract. You will never think of making the person dependent. You will never be so cruel – if you love – as to destroy the freedom of the other. You will help, you will make his sky bigger.

There is only one criterion of love: It gives freedom, and it gives unconditionally.

You have experienced love for the first time. But it is not too late, although you are sixty-three years old. Love transforms old age into youth. If you can go on loving to the very last breath, you will remain young. Love knows no old age. Love knows no death. If you can go on loving, your love will continue beyond death too. Love is the most precious experience in life.

The Golden Future.

CHAPTER 9

You Have Lived Many Times

In Western society, at least, youth is considered to be everything. But the natural corollary of that is, that as one moves away from youth, birthdays are no longer a cause for congratulations, but are an embarassing and unavoidable fact of life. It becomes impolite to ask someone their age; grey hair is dyed, teeth capped or replaced entirely, demoralized breasts and faces have to be lifted, tummies made taut, and varicose veins supported – but under cover. You certainly don't take it as a compliment if someone tells you that you look your age. Would You speak on growing older?

The Western mind is conditioned by the idea that you have only one life – seventy years of age; youth will never come again. In the West, the spring comes only once; naturally, a deep desire to cling as long as possible, to pretend in every possible way that you are still young....

But in the East, the idea was that life is not just one small piece of seventy years in which youth comes only once. The idea was that just as in existence everything moves eternally, the summer comes, the rains come, the winter comes, and the summer again... everything moves like a wheel. Life is not an exception.

Death is the end of one wheel and the beginning of another. Again you will be a child, and again you will be a young woman, and again you will be old. It has been so since the beginning, and it is going to be to the very end... till you become so enlightened that you can jump out of the vicious circle, and can enter into a totally different law: from individuality, you can jump into the universal.

So, one thing: because of the idea of one single life, the West has become too concerned about being young. And then everything is done to remain young as long as possible, to prolong the process. That creates hypocrisy, and that destroys an authentic growth, and that does not allow you to become really wise in your old age because you hate old age.... Because old age reminds you only of death, nothing else; because old age means the full stop is not far away. You have come to the terminus; just one whistle more and the train will stop.

People are trying to remain young, but they don't know that the very fear of losing youth does not allow you to live it in its totality.

And secondly, the fear of losing youth does not allow you to accept old age with grace. You miss both youth – its joy, its intensity – and you also miss the grace, and the wisdom and the peace that old age brings. But the whole thing is based on a false conception of life.

Unless the West changes the idea that there is only one life, this hypocrisy and this clinging and this fear cannot be changed. And in fact, life is not one; you have lived many times, and you will live many times more. Hence, live each moment as totally as possible; there is no hurry to jump for another moment. Time is not money, time is inexhaustible; and it is available to the poor as much as to the rich. The rich are not richer as far as time is concerned, and the poor are not poorer.

Life is an eternal incarnation.

What appears on the surface is very deep rooted in the religions of the West. They are very miserly in giving you only seventy years; and if you try to work it out, almost one third of your life will be lost in sleep; one third of your life will have to be wasted in earning food, clothes, housing. Whatever little is left has to be given to education, football matches, movies, stupid quarrels, fights. If you can save in seventy year's time, seven minutes for yourself, I will count you a wise man.

But it is difficult even to save seven minutes in your whole life. How can you find yourself, and how can you know the mystery of your being, of your life? How can you understand that death is not an end?

Because you have missed experiencing life itself, you are going to miss the great experience of death too; otherwise, there is nothing to be afraid of in death. It is a beautiful sleep, a dreamless sleep; a sleep that is needed for you to move into another body – silently and peacefully. It is a surgical phenomenon, it is almost like anesthesia. Death is a friend, not a foe; and once you understand death as a friend, and start living life without any fear – that it is only a very small time span of seventy years....

If your perspective opens to the eternity of your life, then everything will slow down; then there is no need to be speedy. In everything people are simply rushing. I have seen people taking their office bag, pushing things into it, kissing their wife – not seeing whether she is their wife or somebody else – saying "Goodbye" to their children.... This is not the way of living. And where are you reaching with this speed?

Speed has become more important than destiny, and speed has become more important because life is so short, and you have to do so many things: unless you do them with speed, you cannot manage. You cannot sit silently even for a few minutes – it seems a wastage. In those few minutes you could have earned a few bucks. Just wasting time, closing your eyes... and what is there inside you?

The West has no tradition of mysticism, it is

extrovert: look outward – there is so much to see – but it is not aware that inside there is not only the skeleton, there is something more within the skeleton. That is your consciousness. And by closing your eyes, you will not come across the skeleton, you will come across your very life source.

The West needs a deep acquaintance with its own life source – then there will be no hurry. One will enjoy when life brings youth, one will enjoy when life brings old age, and one will enjoy when life brings death. One simply knows one thing – how to enjoy everything that one comes across, how to transform it into a celebration.

I call it the authentic religion – the art of transforming everything into a celebration, into a song, into a dance.

The Golden Future, Session 16.

CHAPTER 10

Fear And Fascination Exist Together

What do You think about the attitude of the priests and the prophets towards women?

These people, who have been thought to be messengers of God, who have been teaching compassion, love, have never considered at all that women are also human.

They are born out of women. Still, they have all shown nauseating disrespect towards womanhood. The reason is very clear. The reason is: they are afraid of women. And it is a psychological truth that you are afraid and at the same time fascinated. Fear and fascination exist together. In fact, the fear is the by-product of fascination.

They are fascinated, which is natural. There is nothing wrong in it, it is absolutely human. But if they want to be a messiah... then they have to fulfill the conditions which the tradition prescribes for them to fulfill, and all the traditions are made up by man. Up to now we have lived in a man-made society in which the woman has not been taken into consideration at all.

Confucius – and the whole of China is influenced by Confucius' thinking – believes that there is no soul in a woman, she is only body; killing a woman is not a murder. So for thousands of years in China, if somebody killed his own wife it was not a crime. It was just as if you want to destroy your chair, your furniture, or anything that belongs to you; you possess it, it is yours, exactly as the woman is yours. You are the possessor; you can kill her. There was no law in China to prevent a husband from killing his wife, and there was no punishment either, because the woman was a thing, not a being.

And Confucius is thought to be one of the wisest men in the world. Now what kind of wisdom is this? He is the founder of Confucianism, but all that Confucius has done is confused the human mind and nothing else.

Every religion is afraid of women, because every religion is afraid of sex.

Every religion is repressive of sex, against sex. Naturally, it is a by-product that every religion has to be against the woman, the woman has to be condemned. If you condemn sex, you are bound to condemn the woman. If you respect the woman – it is a corollary – you will respect sex also, as a natural thing.

And why were these people against sex? They are different in their attitudes about everything except sex. About sex all religions agree; that seems to be the only agreement amongst religions. So it seems to be tremendously important that we should go deep into the whole phenomenon of why they are afraid of it. They are afraid of sex because it is the greatest energy in man, the most powerful pull of nature and biology. There is no way to destroy it.

Either you can condemn and repress sex or you can understand and transform it. But the second is a long and arduous path and needs tremendous intelligence, awareness – because sex is an unconscious force in you. Each cell in your body is made of it, is vibrant with it. Your conscious mind is nothing compared to your unconscious sexual energy; hence the fear that the unconscious can take possession of you any moment. To repress seems to be easier. Repression needs no intelligence in the first place; any idiot can do it. In fact, only idiots do it.

I have been surprised, seeing hundreds of monks in India belonging to different religions – they are all repressing their sexuality. My surprise was that the more they repress their sexuality, the more stupid they become, exactly in the same proportion. Repressing nature is such an idiotic effort that it is bound to destroy your intelligence. I have found these people so dull. I would be talking to them and I could see they have not heard anything; their eyes look almost dead, their bodies have shrunken. They look ugly. They have been against sex, that's why they have to be against the woman.

Jainas believe that nobody can be liberated from a woman's body. Only man can be liberated, can attain to the ultimate – their word is "moksha" – but only from a man's body, not from a woman's body. What is wrong with a woman's body? There is no difference at all. The only difference is physiological, and that too is not much of a difference – not a difference that can make a difference.

Man's sexual organs are hanging out and woman's sexual organs are hanging in; that's the only difference. Just turn your pocket and let it hang out; the pocket becomes male. Put it back to its original position, it becomes female. This you call a difference? The same pocket? (...) Jainas say a woman is condemned by her female body. First she has to become a man. So there are Jaina nuns – they are not striving for liberation, they are striving to be born in the next life as a man, then they will work for liberation. There is one step more for them than for a man. "Ladies first" does not apply.

One woman in the history of the Jainas must have been a woman of tremendous courage, intelligence, and a rebel; she rebelled against this idea. Her name was Mallibhai. She simply rebelled against this whole idea; she said, "This is just created by man." And she must have been a charismatic woman, certainly, to become a Jaina monk. She was not going to become a nun, because a nun has the goal to become a monk in the next life: she became a Jaina monk. A Jaina nun is allowed to have clothes, she is not to be in the nude; that stage will come in the next life, if she succeeds.

But this woman "Mallibhai" was a rare rebel. I have looked all around the world – I don't find another woman of the same rebelliousness. She became a monk. She dropped her clothes and she declared to the Jainas, "I am a monk and I am striving for liberation, and I don't care a bit what your scriptures say." She was certainly charismatic, and she fulfilled all the requirements that are prescribed for a tirthankara, and the Jainas had to accept her as a tirthankara.

But they played a trick. When she died they changed her name: Mallibhai – "bhai" designates a woman; they made the name Mallinath – "nath" designates a man. So if you read the history, you will not find in twenty-four tirthankaras that there has been a woman, because for her name they don't say Mallibhai, they say Mallinath. They have deceived the whole world, and they have continued on the old trip. One woman has proved it, and one woman's proof is enough for all women. But the cunning priesthood changed the name when she died. They not only changed her name, they changed the statue. It is a man's statue in the temples; in Jaina temples there are twenty-four tirthankaras' statues – all men!

I used to go to Jaina temples and ask, "Who is Mallibhai?"

And the priest would become shaky and he would say, "Er… Mallibhai? Are you a Jaina?"

I would say, "No, I am not a Jaina, but I am not a male chauvinist either. Who is Mallibhai out of these twenty-four?" – and he would show me.

But I would say, "This is a man's statue – the sexual organs are hanging out."

Soon they became aware... so whenever I would go to a Jaina temple they would say, "The temple is closed. You are not allowed in the temple."

It is a male chauvinist world. All Hindu avataras are men; not a single woman is accepted. Not that there have not been women of much more strength, of much more power than these so-called avataras, but they have not been accepted just because they are women, and it is a man's world.

A Mohammedan can marry four women; he is allowed to by the Koran. A woman is not allowed to marry four men. Now this is unjust. A woman cannot enter into the Mohammedan mosque – she has to pray from the outside. She is filthy, just because she is a woman; she is not even allowed to pray inside the mosque. In a synagogue, there is a separate place for the woman, partitioned; she cannot sit with the man. Mostly at the back she has a place, or on the balcony she has a place.

I am reminded of a story – I don't know whether it is right or wrong. When Golda Meir was prime minister of Israel, Indira Gandhi, who was prime minister of India, went on a visit to Israel. She wanted to see a synagogue and how the Jews worship and what they do. So Golda Meir took Indira Gandhi and they sat on the balcony.

Indira Gandhi asked Golda Meir, "Is it a rule of the synagogue that only prime ministers can sit on the balcony?" – because Golda Meir and Indira Gandhi both were women. Golda Meir did not want to say that in the Jewish tradition the woman is kept separate. But Indira Gandhi thought, "It is because we are both prime ministers, so a special place is being given to us." Yes, it was a special place, but not for prime ministers – it was for two women. Even though they are prime ministers, it doesn't matter – a woman is a woman.

The Rajneesh Bible, Volume I, Chapter 6 (excerpts).

CHAPTER 11

No Birth Control, No Abortion: Global Suicide

Why is the church so much
against abortion and
birth control?

Politics is a game of numbers. How many Christians you have in the world – that is your power. The more Christians there are, the more power is in the hands of Christian priests, the priesthood. Nobody is interested in saving anybody, but just in increasing the population. What Christianity has been doing is continually issuing orders from the Vatican against birth control, saying it is sin to use birth control methods; it is sin to believe in abortion or to propagate abortion, or to make it legal.

Do you think they are interested in the unborn children? They are not interested – they have nothing to do with those unborn children. They pursue their interest knowing perfectly well that if abortion is not practiced, if birth control methods are not practiced, then this whole humanity is going to commit a global suicide. And it is not so far away that you cannot see the situation. Within just fifteen years the world population will be such that it will be impossible to survive.

But just now, just recently, the Vatican has come out with a long message to humanity – one hundred and thirty-nine pages; "Abortion is sin. Birth control is sin." Now, nowhere in the Bible is abortion sin. Nowhere in the Bible is birth control sin, because no birth control was needed. Out of ten children, nine were going to die. That was the proportion, and that was the proportion in India just thirty or forty years ago: out of ten children, only one would survive. That was perfectly okay. Then the population was not too great, not too heavy on the resources of the earth. Now, even in India – not to say anything about developed countries – even in India, out of ten children, only one dies.

So on one hand medical science goes on helping people to survive and Christianity goes on opening hospitals and distributing medicines, and Mother Teresa is there to praise you and the Pope is going to bless you.... There are all kinds of associations – they are even worried about Russia. There is, in America, a Christian association called "Underground Evangelism," which works in communist countries to distribute Bibles freely and to distribute these stupid ideas that abortion is sin and birth control is sin.

Somehow Russia is not starving; they are not rich but they are not starving. Please, at least leave them alone. And it is because of birth control that they are not starving. If birth control is prohibited, if abortion is prohibited, Russia will be in the same position as Ethiopia. Then Mother Teresa will be very happy. The underground evangelists will come overground – a great opportunity to convert people to Christianity.

The Rajneesh Bible, Volume III, Chapter 18 (excerpts).

CHAPTER 12

A Woman Is Hurting In The Deepest Core Of Her Being

In *The Prophet* by Kahlil Gibran, a woman asks Almustafa to speak about pain. Would You comment on this excerpt?

And a woman spoke, saying, Tell us of Pain.

And Almustafa said:

Your pain is the breaking of the shell that encloses your understanding.

Even as the stone of the fruit must break, that its heart may stand in the sun, so must you know pain.

And could you keep your heart in wonder at the daily miracles of your life, your pain would not seem less wondrous than your joy;

And you would accept the seasons of your heart, even as you have always accepted the seasons that pass over your fields.

And you would watch with serenity through the winters of your grief.

Much of your pain is self-chosen.

It is the bitter potion by which the physician within you heals your sick self.

Therefore trust the physician, and drink his remedy in silence and tranquillity:

For his hand, though heavy and hard, is guided by the tender hand of the Unseen,

And the Cup he brings, though it burn your lips,

has been fashioned of the clay which the Potter has moistened with His own sacred tears.

It seems that it is very difficult, even for a man of Kahlil Gibran's calibre, to forget a deep-rooted, male chauvinistic attitude. I am saying this because the statements that Almustafa is going to make are right in a way – still they miss something very essential.

Almustafa forgets that the question is raised by a woman, and his answer is very general, applicable to both man and woman. But the truth is that the pain and suffering that women of the world have gone through is a thousand fold more than man has ever known.

That's why I say Almustafa is answering the question but not the questioner. And unless the questioner is answered, the answer remains superficial – howsoever profound it may sound. I would like you to remember again and again: Wherever I see that just a small sentence or sometimes just even a word would have made it more true, far deeper, far more compassionate....

The answer seems to be academic, philosophic. It does not have the insight into what man has done to the woman – and it is not a question of one day... for thousands of years. He does not even mention it. On the contrary, he goes on doing the same that the priests and the politicians have always been doing: giving consolations. Behind beautiful words there is nothing but consolation – and consolation cannot be a substitute for truth.

"And a woman spoke...." Is it not strange that out of that whole crowd no man asked about pain? Is it just accidental? No, absolutely no. It is very relevant that a woman asked the question, "Tell us of pain," because only the woman knows how many wounds she has been carrying, how much slavery – physical, mental and spiritual – she has suffered and is still suffering.

A woman is hurting in the deepest core of her being. No man knows the depth pain can go into you and destroy your dignity, your pride, your very humanity.

Almustafa said, "Your pain is the breaking of the shell that encloses your understanding." A very poor statement, so superficial that I feel ashamed of Kahlil Gibran sometimes. Any idiot can say it. It is not worthy of Kahlil Gibran. "Your pain is the breaking of the shell that encloses your understanding." It is a very simple and general statement.

"Even as the stone of the fruit must break, that its heart may stand in the sun, so must you know pain." I hate this statement. He is supporting the idea that you must experience pain. It is a truism, but not a truth. It is very factual – a seed has to go in great suffering because unless the seed dies in his suffering the tree will never be born, and the great foliage and the beauty of the flowers will never come into existence. But who remembers the seed and its courage to die for the unknown to be born?

The same is true – unless the shell that encloses your understanding goes through suffering, breaks down, allows freedom to your understanding, there is going to be a certain pain. But what is the shell? That's how poets have escaped from crucifixions. He should have explained what the shell is.

All the knowledge, all your conditionings, the whole

process of your upbringing, your education, your society and civilization – they constitute the shell which keeps you and your understanding imprisoned. But he is not mentioning a single word of what he means by "shell." If he had said, "Your religion, your philosophy, your political ideology, your nationality, your race – these are all constituents of your imprisonment," instead of having international respect, honor, he would have been condemned by all the religions, by all the nations, by all the races, which means by almost the whole world.

Almustafa is saying, "Your pain is the breaking of the shell that encloses your understanding." It is true, but it would have been more sincere if he had explained what he means by "the shell," because the whole thing depends on the meaning of the word "shell." What is the shell?

People will read it just like fiction, poetry, and nobody will ever take note that they have passed the word "shell," which contains your whole past. And unless you are ready to disconnect yourself from your past, there is going to be pain. It is your past – it is not easy just to get out of it. It is not like clothes that you can change, it is like peeling your skin. But without passing through this pain there is no possibility of any understanding.

This is true for both men and women, but it is more true for women because the whole past is created by the male. The female has been simply a shadow, not very substantial. All Hindu incarnations of God are men. It is so surprising and shocking that they can accept animals as the incarnations of God, but they have not accepted a single woman as an incarnation of God.

The woman has been completely ignored; has not been taken into account at all. She constitutes half of the world, and for thousands of years she has had no voting right.

In China it has been believed that she has no soul, so the question of pain does not arise. If you destroy your furniture do you think the furniture will go through great suffering? That there will be pain? If you slap the table do you think there will be tears? China, for centuries, has categorized woman with things; hence, in the Chinese morality, to murder your own wife is not a crime. It is your wife, it is your possession; you can do anything you want to do.

In India.... Gautam Buddha is a man; his great disciples – Mahakashyap, Sariputta, Moggalayan – all are men. Was there not a single woman who could have been raised to the same consciousness? But Gautam Buddha himself was denying initiation to women: They are a species not of humanity but of some subhuman state. Why bother with them? – let them first attain manhood.

The statement of Gautam Buddha is that man is the crossroads from where you can go anywhere – to enlightenment, to ultimate freedom – but the woman is not mentioned at all. She is not a crossroads but just a dark street where no municipal corporation has even put lights. It goes nowhere. Man is a superhighway. So first let the woman come on the superhighway; let her become a man, be born in the body of a man – then there is some possibility of her becoming enlightened.

Says Almustafa, "... so you must know pain" – but

for what? If the woman cannot become enlightened, why should she go through pain? She is not gold, in that going through fire she will become purer.

"And could you keep your heart in wonder at the daily miracles of your life, your pain would not seem less wondrous than your joy...." It is true, but sometimes truth can be very dangerous, a double-edged sword. On one hand it protects, on another hand it destroys. It is true that if you keep the wonder in your eyes you will be surprised to know that even pain has its own sweetness, its own miracle, its own joy. It is not less wondrous than joy itself.

But the strange fact is that the woman is always more like a child, more full of wonder than man. Man is always after knowledge – and what is knowledge? Knowledge is just a means to get rid of wonder. The whole of science is trying to demystify existence. And it is a very simple fact that the more you know, the less you wonder.

But Almustafa does not mention the fact that women always remain closer to the child than men. That is one part of their beauty: their innocence – they don't know. Man has never allowed them to know anything. They know small things – about keeping the house and the kitchen and taking care of the children and the husband – but these are not the things that can prevent.... This is not great knowledge, this can be put aside very easily.

That's why, whenever a woman has come to listen to me, she has heard me more deeply, more intimately, more lovingly. But when a new man comes to hear me, he is very resistant, alert; afraid that he may be influenced, hurt if his knowledge is not supported; or, if hc is very cunning, he goes on interpreting whatever is said according to his own knowledge. And he will say, "I know it all – there was nothing new."

This is a measure to protect his ego, to protect the hard shell; and unless that shell breaks and you find yourself wondering like a child, there is no possibility of your ever being in a space which we have always known as the soul, your very being.

And this has been my experience all over the world – that the woman listens, and you can see the glitter of wonder in her eyes. It is not superficial, its roots are deep into her heart.

But Kahlil Gibran does not mention the fact, although the question is asked by a woman. In fact man is even so cowardly that he is afraid to ask questions – because your question proves your ignorance. All the best questions in *The Prophet* you will find are asked by women: about love, about marriage, about children, about pain. Authentic, real – not about God, not about any philosophical system, but about life itself. They may not look like great questions but they are really the greatest questions, and the person who can solve them has entered into a new world.

But Almustafa answers as if the question has been asked by anybody – X Y Z; he is not answering the questioner. And my approach is always that the real question is the questioner. Why has it arisen in a woman and not in a man? – because the woman has suffered slavery; the woman has suffered humiliation; the woman has suffered economic dependence; and above all she has suffered a constant state of pregnancy – for centuries. She has lived in pain and pain and pain.

The growing child in her does not allow her to eat; she is always feeling like throwing up, vomiting. And when the child has grown to nine months, the birth of the child is almost the death of the woman. And she is not even free of one pregnancy and the husband is ready to make her pregnant again. It seems that the woman's only function is to be a factory to produce crowds.

And what is man's function? He does not participate in her pain. Nine months she suffers, the birth of the child she suffers; and what does the man do? As far as the man is concerned he simply uses the woman as an object to fulfill his lust and sexuality. He is not concerned at all about what the consequence will be for the woman, and still he goes on saying, "I love you." If he has really loved her the world would not have been overpopulated. His word "love" is absolutely empty: he has treated her almost like cattle.

And you would accept the seasons of your heart, even as you have always accepted the seasons that pass over your fields....

True, and yet not absolutely true: true, if you forget about the questioner, but not true if you remember the questioner.

Just as a philosophical statement it is true: "And you would accept the seasons of your heart...." Sometimes there is pleasure and sometimes there is pain and sometimes there is just indifference, no pain, no pleasure. He is saying, "If you accept the seasons of your heart, even as you have always accepted the seasons that pass over your fields...."

Superficially it is true. Acceptance of anything gives you a certain peace, a certain calmness. You are not too much worried, you know this too will pass. But as far as the woman is concerned there is a difference. She is constantly living in one season: pain and pain. The seasons don't change from summer to winter... or to rain. The woman's life is really hard.

It is not so hard today, but only in the advanced countries. In the so-called developing countries – which are not really developing, which are really undeveloped countries. Only the word has been changed. They used to be called "undeveloped" countries; and this is the cunningness of human mind, that the word "undeveloped" hurts – so, "developing countries" to hide the fact that nothing is developing.

Eighty percent of India's population lives in villages, where you can see the real hardship that the woman goes through. She has been going through that hardship for centuries, and the season does not change. If you look into this fact then this statement becomes anti revolutionary. Then this statement becomes a consolation: "Accept the slavery of man, accept the torture of the man."

The woman has lived in such pain, and yet Almustafa completely forgets who is asking the question. It is possible to accept the change of seasons, but not ten thousand years of slavery. The season does not change....

The woman needs revolt, not acceptance.

Man is the most lustful animal on the earth. Every

animal has a season when the male becomes interested in the female. Sometimes the season is only for a few weeks, sometimes a month or two months, and then for the whole year they forget all about sex; they forget all about reproduction. That's why they are not in a situation of overpopulation. It is only man who is sexual all the year round. And if he is American then he is sexual in the night, he is sexual in the morning.

And you are asking the woman to accept the pain.

I cannot ask my people to accept such pain, pain which is imposed by others on you.

You need a revolution. (...)

"And you would watch with serenity through the winters of your grief...." Why? When we can change it, why should we watch? Watch only that which cannot be changed. Watch only that which is natural – be a witness to it. But this is poetic cunningness, beautiful words: "And watch with serenity...." And what about Kahlil Gibran beating his own wife? "Watch with serenity!"

Watch anything that is natural with serenity, and revolt against all suffering that is imposed by anybody. Whether it is a man or woman, whether it is your father or mother, whether it is the priest or the professor, whether it is the government or the society – revolt! Unless you have a rebellious spirit you are not alive in the true sense of the word.

"Much of your pain is self chosen...." This is true. All your misery, all your pain – much of it is not imposed by others. Against that which is imposed by others, revolt; but that which you have chosen yourself, drop it. There is no need to watch. Just the understanding that "I have imposed it upon myself" is enough – throw it away. Let others watch, you throw it! Seeing you throwing it away, perhaps they will also understand: "Why unnecessarily suffer? – the neighbors are throwing away their grief."

Your jealousies, your anger, your greed – they all bring pain. Your ambitions, they all bring pain. And they are self-chosen.

"It is the bitter potion by which the physician within you heals your sick self." Again he comes back to console you. He is not making a clear-cut distinction that there are pains which are imposed by others – revolt against them – and there are pains which are natural: witness them, and witness them with serenity, because it is the bitter medicine with which the physician, nature, within you heals your sick self.

"Therefore trust the physician, and drink his remedy in silence and tranquillity…." But remember it is about the physician, not about your husband, not about the government. They impose pain over you, not to heal you but to destroy you, to crush you, because the more you are destroyed, the more easily you can be dominated; there is no fear of rebellion from your side. So remember who the physician is. Nature heals, time heals: you simply wait, witness. But be very clear what is natural and what is artificial.

Whatever is natural, whatever is, against which no rebellion is possible – then don't be miserable; then accept it with gratitude. It is the invisible hand of the divine which wants to heal you, which wants to bring you to a higher state of consciousness. But whatever is unnatural – to yield to any kind of slavery is to destroy your own soul. It is better to die than to live as a slave.

The Messiah, Volume II, Session 4.

CHAPTER 13

A Slave Cannot Be A Friend

Nietzsche says, in
Thus Spake Zarathustra
that woman is incapable of
friendship. Would You comment?

Friendship has been one of the subjects most ignored by almost all the philosophers. Perhaps we take it for granted that we understand what it means; hence we have remained ignorant about its depths, about its possibilities of growth, about its different colors with different significances.

The most important thing to remember is: one needs friends because one is incapable of being alone. And as long as one needs friends, one cannot be much of a friend – because the need reduces the other to an object. Only the man who is capable of being alone is also capable of being a friend. But it is not his need, it is his joy; it is not his hunger, not his thirst, but his abundance of love that he wants to share.

When such a friendship exists, it should not be called a friendship, because it has taken a totally new dimension: I call it "friendliness." It has gone beyond relationship... because all relationships are bondages in some way or other. They make you a slave and they enslave others. Friendliness is simply the joy of sharing without any conditions, without any expectations, with no desire that something should be returned – not even gratefulness.

Friendliness is the purest kind of love.

It is not a need, it is not a necessity:

It is sheer abundance, overflowing ecstasy.

Zarathustra says, "Our faith in others betrays wherein we would dearly like to have faith in ourselves."

A man who believes in others is a man who is afraid to believe in himself. The Christian, the Hindu, the Mohammedan, the Buddhist, the communist – nobody is courageous enough to have faith in his own being. He believes in others, and he believes in those who believe in him.

It is really ridiculous: your friend needs you, he is afraid of his aloneness; you need him, because you are afraid of your aloneness. Both are afraid of aloneness. Do you think your being together means your aloneness will disappear? It will simply be doubled, or perhaps multiplied; hence all relationships lead into more misery, into more anguish. Nobody can satisfy your emptiness.

You pave to encounter your emptiness.

You have to live it, you have to accept it.

And in your acceptance is hidden a great revolution, a great revelation.

The moment you accept your aloneness, your emptiness, its very quality changes. It becomes just its opposite – it becomes an abundance, a fulfillment, an overflowing of energy and joy. Out of this overflowing, if your trust arises it has meaning; if your friendliness arises it is significant; if your love arises it is not just a word, it is your very heart.

The desire to have faith in someone betrays only one thing: you are too poor, too empty, too unconscious.

And this is not the way to change your situation; this is simply the way to a false consolation.

You don't need consolation; you need a revolution, you need a transformation of your being. You have to come to terms with yourself – that is the first step in having the right trust, the right friendship, the right love. Otherwise all your relationships – of love, of friendship, of faith – are nothing but betrayals. You are exposing yourself and declaring that you are empty, unworthy, undeserving.

If you cannot love yourself, who is going to love you?

If you cannot be a friend to yourself, who is going to be a friend to you?

If you cannot trust in yourself, who is going to trust you?

You yourself are a slave, but you pretend to be a deliverer to your friend. And the same is true about your so-called saviors: they themselves are not saved, but they are ready to save the whole world. Even in the twentieth century, at the very end, millions of people are still believing that all that they need to do is to believe in Jesus – that he is the only begotten son of God – and then they can go on doing anything they want, they will be saved. Very cheap – just believe.

The first night when I was forced into the jail in America.... The other prisoner in my cell must have been a very devout Christian. He had The Bible on his bed, and kneeling down on the ground, he put his head on The Bible very piously. And just above The Bible there were all kinds of pornographic pictures, cut out from magazines, that he had pasted all over the wall. I watched the whole thing, and when he had finished his prayer, I asked him, "Who has put these pictures here? They are really beautiful."

He said, "I have done it – do you like them?"

I said, "They are so beautiful. I am also a pious man." That made him a little suspicious, when I said, "I am also a pious man."

He said, "What do you mean by that?"

I said, "Can't you see the contradiction? You are praying to God, putting your head on The Bible, kneeling down on the ground, hoping that you will be saved...."

He said, "Certainly I will be saved. I am a believer in God, I am a believer in Jesus Christ."

And I said, "What about these pornographic pictures?"

He said, "That does not matter. Once you believe in Jesus, you are saved."

I said, "Perhaps that's why.... How many times have you been in jail?"

He said, "This is only the fourth time."

"And what kind of crimes have you been committing?"

He said, "All kinds. But I always pray in the morning and in the night – jail or no jail. These are small things. My belief in Jesus is absolute; he cannot go against his promise."

I said, "Do you have any guarantee? If he does not

appear on the last judgment day, you will be in trouble. If all these naked girls appear and they say, 'He is our follower. He has been kneeling before us every morning, every evening....'"

He looked at me. He was angry; he said, "It seems you are not a Christian."

I said, "I am a Christian; otherwise, why should I bother about you? But you are bowing down before these naked girls in different pornographic, obscene pictures. All these girls will appear on the last judgment day and I will be there, you remember, as an eyewitness."

He said, "My God! I have heard about you, I have seen you on television, and they say, perhaps rightly, that you are a dangerous man. Forgive me, but don't mention these pictures on the last day."

I said, "You take them down."

He said, "That's a little difficult. I cannot pray twenty-four hours, and that is my only entertainment – cutting from magazines, putting them all over.... And not that I alone am doing it, all the cells in the prison are full of pornographic pictures." The jail provides all these magazines for the prisoners and the jail also provides The Bible.

The next day when the jailer came I asked him, "You are providing both these things for these poor inmates of the jail – can't you see the contradiction?"

He said, "Nobody ever pointed out the contradiction." I said, "Do you need that somebody should point it out? You cannot see it yourself?"

He told me, "You come with me into the office.

There we can discuss it, not before the prisoners – you can provoke them."

I said, "I am not provoking them against The Bible, I am provoking them against these ugly pictures that are all over the walls. You come round every day and you see all this happening, and you are silent about it. I will expose you also to the media when I get out."

He said, "Don't do that!"

I said, "That's what that prisoner was saying to me, 'Don't do that on judgment day.'"

There are people who are not aware of their deep tendency to be slaves. They want to be enslaved, because while they are enslaved all their responsibilities are taken by the person who enslaves them.

Unless you are ready to take all the responsibilities of life, something in you will always want to be a slave, because only the slave is free of responsibilities. But a slave cannot be a friend – he is searching for a master, not a friend. And the same is true from the other side... because you are in search of slaves, you are not in search of friends. And anybody who has dignity is not going to be enslaved in the name of friendship. Zarathustra says, "In woman, a slave and a tyrant have all too long been concealed."

The responsibility goes to the man. Zarathustra has not mentioned it. Perhaps he still thinks of himself only as a man – he has not transcended the duality of man and woman. He talks about women as a man; hence he takes no responsibility. Otherwise, for much that is wrong in women, the responsibility goes to the man. Man has forced her. He has made her almost a doll –

just a showpiece. He has not given her the same respect that he asks from her to be given to him. He has forced her to be spiritually a slave, and naturally there has been in women, for thousands of years, a burning desire for revenge.

It comes out in small ways: she tortures the husband, nags him, is continually bitchy. But the responsibility, I want you to remember, is man's. The woman has not been given freedom. You have made her a slave, and she wants to get out of that slavery, but you have broken all the bridges around her.

You have not allowed her to be educated, you have not allowed her free movement in society, you have not allowed her financial freedom... and you have kept her continuously pregnant. You have used her. You have not given her the respect a human being deserves – naturally there is vengeance.

And she takes her revenge in her own ways: she tortures you, she makes your life a hell. You have made her life a hell; she makes your life a hell. Your ways and her ways are different, but the ultimate outcome is that you both live in a hell.

Woman is not capable of friendship because she is not free; her individuality is not recognized; her independence is not respected – how can she be a friend?

And if she cannot even know friendship, how can she know love? She knows only lust. And she hates the man for the same reason, because she knows perfectly well that all these sweet words – "darling" and "honey" and "I love you" – are nothing but prefaces for lust. And naturally she reacts in her own way – that she has a headache. You are saying "darling" and "honey," and she is saying she has a headache. She has her own ways to torture you – you have tortured her enough.

Still, woman's love is more insightful than anything else in her. Her logic has been destroyed by man, her intelligence has been spoiled by man; only her love.... Although every effort has been made down the centuries so that she simply remains a useful instrument for man's sexuality, still her love has remained intact.

But this is the problem: it is very difficult for even men like Gautam Buddha and Zarathustra to rise above their manhood. The woman remains something of the lower, not belonging to the height of man. She remains somewhere down in the dark valleys.

If there is anything alive in woman, in spite of man's continuous violence against her, it is her love. Her love is in her eyes, her love is her whole being.

And that is the only hope for woman's liberation. That is the only hope for women to attain, for the first time in history, their dignity, their uniqueness, their spiritual growth. They are in no way inferior to any man.

Zarathustra says, "And in the enlightened love of a woman too, there is still the unexpected attack and lightning and night, along with the light."

The responsibility again is of the man. A man and a woman can remain at peace only when their equality and their uniqueness becomes an accepted phenomenon. Then friendship can flower. Then the night and the unexpected attack will disappear.

The woman has been driven almost crazy by man. It is a great miracle that she has survived amongst a society in which all the religions are man-made, all the governments are man-made, all the laws are man-made, all the societies are man-made, all the educational systems are man-made. How has the woman survived? That is a miracle.

As far as I understand, this miracle has been possible because of her love. Even though man has mistreated her, she has still loved him. Even though she has been enslaved and chained, she has remained a mother, a sister, a beloved, a daughter.

Her survival, against so much attack on her personality, is possible only because existence needs her more than it needs man. Existence has been protective of woman because woman is the mother, from where all life flows. It is through her love that life can still sing, can still dance, that there is still some beauty and there is still some grace left in the world.

Women constitute half of the population of the world. If they are liberated, given their basic birthrights, the world will go into a tremendous metamorphosis – which it needs tremendously.

Woman has been prevented from contributing anything, except children. She can contribute so much, and its quality will be totally different. It will have more beauty, it will have more aliveness, it will have more love, it will have more juice.

Zarathustra: A God That Can Dance, (Session 11).

CHAPTER 14

Tantra Has Never Been Male Chauvinistic

What is Tantra?

The most basic thing about Tantra is this – and it is very radical, revolutionary, rebellious – the basic vision is that the world is not divided into the lower and the higher, but that the world is one piece. The higher and the lower are holding hands. The higher includes the lower, and the lower includes the higher. The higher is hidden in the lower, so the lower has not to be denied, has not to be condemned, has not to be destroyed or killed. The lower has to be transformed.

Poison and nectar are two phases of the same energy, so are life and death – and so is everything: day and night, love and hate, sex and superconsciousness.

Tantra says: Never condemn anything – the attitude of condemnation is a stupid attitude. By condemning something you are denying yourself the possibility that would have become available to you if you had evolved the lower. Don't condemn the mud, because the lotus is hidden in the mud: use the mud to produce the lotus. Of course the mud is not the lotus yet, but it can be. And the creative person, the religious person, will help the mud to release its lotus so that the lotus can be freed from the mud.

Saraha is the founder of the Tantra vision. Tantra is of tremendous import, and particularly for the present moment in human history, because a new man is striving to be born, a new consciousness is knocking on the doors. And the future is going to be that of Tantra, because now no more dual attitudes can hold man's mind.

They have tried for centuries and they have crippled man and they have made man guilty. They have not made man free; they have made man a prisoner. They have not made man happy either; they have made man very miserable. They have condemned everything. From food to sex they have condemned everything: from relationship to friendship they have condemned all. Love is condemned, the body is condemned, the mind is condemned. They have not left a single inch for you to stand on: they have taken away all, and man is hanging, just hanging.

This state of man cannot be tolerated any more. Tantra can give you a new perspective.

You may not even have heard the name of Saraha, but Saraha is one of the great benefactors of humanity. A few things about Saraha's life. He was the son of a very learned brahmin who was in the court of King Mahapala.

The king was willing to give his own daughter to Saraha, but Saraha wanted to renounce all – Saraha wanted to become a sannyasin. He became a disciple of Sri Kirti.

One day while Saraha was meditating, suddenly he saw a vision – a vision that there was a woman in the marketplace who was going to be his real teacher. Sri Kirti had put him on the way, but the real teaching was to come from a woman. Now, this too has to be understood. It is only Tantra that has never been male chauvinistic. In fact, to go into Tantra you will need the cooperation of a wise woman; without a wise woman you will not be able to enter into the complex world of Tantra.

He saw a vision: a woman there in the marketplace. So first a woman. Second – in the marketplace. Tantra thrives in the marketplace, in the thick of life. It is not an attitude of negation, it is utter positivity. (...) He went to the marketplace. He was surprised: he really found the woman that he had seen in the vision. The woman was making an arrow – she was an arrowsmith woman.

The third thing to be remembered about Tantra: it says the more cultured, the more civilized a person, the less is the possibility of his Tantric transformation. The less civilized, the more primitive, the more alive a person is. The more you become civilized, the more you become plastic – you become artificial, you become too cultivated, you lose your roots into the earth. You are afraid of the muddy world. You start living away from the world; you start posing yourself as though you are not of the world. Tantra says: to find the real person you will have to go to the roots.

An arrowsmith woman is a low-caste woman, and for Saraha – a learned brahmin, a famous brahmin, who had belonged to the court of the king – going to an arrowsmith woman is symbolic.

The learned has to go to the vital.

The plastic has to go to the real.

He saw this woman, a young woman – very alive, radiant with life – cutting an arrow-shaft, looking neither to the right nor to the left, but wholly absorbed in making the arrow. He immediately felt something extraordinary in her presence, something that he had never come across. Even Sri Kirti, his master, paled before the presence of this woman. Something so fresh and something from the very source....

Saraha watched carefully. The arrow ready, the woman closing one eye and opening the other, assumed the posture of aiming at an invisible target. Saraha came still closer. Now, there was no target, she was simply posing. She had closed one eye, her other eye was open, and she was aiming at some unknown target – invisible, it was not there. Saraha started feeling some message. The posture was symbolic, he felt, but still it was very dim and dark. He could feel something there, but he could not figure it out, what it was.

So he asked the woman whether she was a professional arrowsmith, and the Woman laughed loudly, a wild laugh, and said, "You stupid brahmin! You have left the Vedas, but now you are worshiping Buddha's sayings, the Dhammapada. So what is the point? – you have changed your books, you have changed your philosophy, but you remain all the time the same stupid man."

Saraha was shocked. Nobody had talked to him that way – only an uncultured woman could talk that way. And the way she laughed was so uncivilized, so primitive – but still, something was very much alive. And he was feeling pulled. She was a great magnet and he was nothing but a piece of iron.

And then she said, "You think you are a Buddhist?"

– he must have been in the robe of the Buddhist monk, be yellow robe – and she laughed again. She said, "Buddha's meaning can only be known through actions, not through words and not through books. Is it not enough for you? Are you not yet fed up with all this? Do not waste any more time in that futile search. Come and follow me!"

And something happened, something like a communion. He had never felt like that before. In that moment, the spiritual significance of what she was doing dawned upon Saraha. Neither looking to the left, nor looking to the right, he had seen her just looking in the middle.

For the first time he understood what Buddha means by being in the middle: avoid the axis. First he was a philosopher, now he has become anti-philosopher – from one extreme to another. First he was worshiping one thing, now he is worshiping just the opposite but the worship continues. You can move from the left to the right, from the right to the left, but that is not going to help. The middle is the point from where the transcendence happens.

For the first time Saraha saw it actually there – he had not even seen it in Sri Kirti. It was really there. And the woman was true, she said, "You can only learn through action." And she was so utterly absorbed that she was not even looking at Saraha who was standing there watching her. She was so utterly absorbed, she was totally in the action. That is again a Buddhist message: to be total in action is to be free of action.

Karma is created because you are not totally in it.

If you are totally in it, it leaves no trace. Do anything totally and it is finished, and you will not carry a psychological memory of it. Do anything incompletely and it hangs with you, it goes on – it is a hangover. And the mind wants to continue and do it and complete it.

Mind has a great temptation to complete things. Complete anything and the mind is gone. If you continue doing things totally, one day you suddenly find there is no mind. Mind is the accumulated past of all incomplete actions.

You wanted to love a woman and you didn't love; now the woman is dead. You wanted to go to your father and you wanted to be forgiven for all that you had been doing, for all that you had been doing in such a way that he was feeling hurt – now he is dead. Now the hangover will remain. Now the ghost.... Now you are helpless – what to do? Whom to go to? And how to ask for forgiveness? You wanted to be kind to a friend but you could not be because you became closed. Now the friend is no more, and it hurts. You start feeling a guilt, you repent. Things go on like this.

Do any action totally and you are free of it, and you don't look back. And the real man never looks back – because there is nothing to see. He has no hangovers. He simply goes ahead. His eyes are clear of the past, his vision is not clouded. In that clarity one comes to know what reality is.

You are so worried with all your incomplete actions; you are like a junkyard. One thing is incomplete here, another thing is incomplete there – nothing is complete. Have you watched it? Have you ever completed anything? Or is everything just incomplete? And you go on pushing aside one thing and you start another thing, and before it is complete you start another. You become more and more burdened – this is what karma is. Karma means incomplete action.

Be total... and you will be free.

The woman was totally absorbed. That's why she was looking so luminous, she was looking so beautiful. She was an ordinary woman, but the beauty was not of this earth. The beauty came because of total absorption. The beauty came because she was not an extremist. The beauty came because she was in the middle, balanced. Out of balance is grace.

For the first time Saraha encountered a woman who was not just physically beautiful, who was spiritually beautiful. Naturally, he was surrendered. The surrender happened. Absorbed totally, absorbed in whatsoever she was doing, he understood for the first time: this is what meditation is. Not that you sit for a special period and repeat a mantra, not that you go to the church or to the temple or to the mosque, but to be in life – to go on doing trivial things, but with such absorption that the profundity is revealed in every action.

He understood what meditation is for the first time. He had been meditating, he had been struggling hard, but for the first time meditation was there, alive. He could feel it. He could have touched it. It was almost tangible. And then he remembered that closing one eye, opening the other, is a symbol, a Buddhist symbol.

Suddenly he realized that the woman had closed one eye: she had closed one eye as symbolic of closing the eye of reason, logic. And she had opened the other eye symbolic of love, intuition, awareness. And then he remembered the posture.

Aiming at the unknown invisible, we are on the journey to know the unknown – to know that which cannot be known. That is real knowledge: to know that which cannot be known, to realize that which is unrealizable, to attain that which cannot be attained. So he remembered the posture. Aiming at the unknown, the invisible, the unknowable, the one – that is the aim. How to be one with existence? The nondual is the aim, where subject and object are lost, where I and thou are lost.

Saraha said to her, "You are not an ordinary arrowsmith woman. I am sorry to have even thought that you were an ordinary arrowsmith woman. Excuse me, I am tremendously sorry. You are a great master, and I am reborn through you. Till yesterday I was not a real brahmin; from today I am. You are my master and you are my mother and you have given me a new birth: I am no more the same."

A disciple and a master – it is a soul love affair. Saraha had found his soulmate. They were in tremendous love, great love, which rarely happens on the earth. She taught him Tantra. Only a woman can teach Tantra. She already has those qualities, those loving, affectionate qualities; she naturally has that care, that love, that feeling for the soft.

Saraha became a tantrika under the guidance of this arrowsmith woman. Now he was no longer meditating. One day he had left all the Vedas, scriptures, knowledge;

now he left even meditation. Now rumors started spreading all over the country: He no longer meditates. He sings, of course, and dances too, but no meditation any more. Now singing was his meditation. Now celebration was his whole lifestyle.

Saraha was no longer serious – Tantra is not. Tantra is a playfulness. Yes, it is sincere, but not serious. It is very joyous. Play entered his being – Tantra is play, because Tantra is a highly evolved form of love: Love is play. Play entered his being – and through play true religion was born.

The Tantra Vision, Volume I, Chapter 1.

CHAPTER 15

Pregnant With Enlightenment

Every great poet knows that when some poetry is striving to be born he feels almost feminine, almost like a womb in which the poetry is taking shape and growing. The same is true of all creative arts; but it is more true about those who are meditating, because they are pregnant with a Gautam Buddha. They are going to give birth to themselves. It is a very mysterious phenomenon, but very like the pregnancy of a woman.

You are saying, "Something is happening to me – a feeling of fullness, richness, and expansion." Those are the symptoms that your old life is going to disappear and a new life is taking shape within you. Where there was emptiness, now there is fullness. Where there was a poverty... because all that man desires, wants, proves only one thing: that he is poor. And you cannot find even the richest man who is not poor in this sense; he may have everything, still he is wanting more. He is a rich poor man, a rich beggar. Your poverty is disappearing and a richness is taking its place.

Everybody lives a closed life. Out of fear – the fear of exposure, the fear of becoming vulnerable, the fear of one's nakedness – one goes on hiding oneself, creating walls and walls around oneself. But as one starts meditating those walls start collapsing, because consciousness needs expansion. It cannot be confined in a small space – even the whole sky is too small for it.

You are going through a great transformation. This is the transformation everyone is here for. You are saying, "This is like a strange pregnancy, which I know nothing about." Now you will know more and more about it. Just avoid abortion! And as far as man is concerned, and his creativity is concerned, no birth control is needed. More and more people have to be in the same state of creativity.

You are wondering, "How can I be? I am a man." That's why you can be – because you are a man. There is a deep psychological background to it which has to be understood. Man has always felt inferior in comparison to woman, because woman can give birth and man cannot. Woman can become a mother – the beginning of a new life; man cannot do it. To substitute for it man started finding in what ways he could also be creative and productive. It was a deep spiritual need to destroy that inferiority.

Man has given birth to great paintings, to great poetry, to great dances, to great music – they are all substitutes.... You may create a beautiful statue, but still it is dead. You may create great music, but it is ephemeral; it comes like the wind and goes away. You may create great dance, but it cannot be a living child, a smiling child – a child who sees, wonders, breathes, whose heart beats.

All your art and all your creativity, seem to be a poor substitute to the woman. I have been asked many times why women are not great poets, great musicians, great painters, great sculptors. The reason is that because they can give birth to life, they don't feel any need to create anything else.

Only on one point, in one place, man and woman meet, and that I call the space of meditation – where man and woman are really equal, because both can give birth to themselves. They can be reborn; both can be pregnant with enlightenment.

Except in the space of meditation, man and woman are two different species. They meet only in deep meditation. And unless the whole humanity is meditative, men and women will go on fighting with each other. Their love is going always up and down – there are moments of beauty, and there are moments of ugliness; there are moments of joy, and there are moments of misery.

But in meditation – if two meditators share their energies – love is a constant phenomenon, it does not change. It has the quality of eternity; it becomes divine. The meeting of love and meditation is the greatest experience in life.

To have love without meditation is to live in a very troubled, anxiety-ridden state – in anguish, angst, always in a turmoil. There are moments of silence, but that silence is nothing but cold war – preparation for another war, that's all. Obviously, to prepare for another war, for a few days, for a few moments, you have to be silent.

But it has not been possible up to now, because all the religions have decided on a wrong path. They have decided to separate men and women; they have decided to make them enemies. And they are all against me because I am trying for a single thing: that as far as meditation is concerned it is nobody's monopoly – neither male nor female. It is the only meeting point, where man is no more a man, nor a woman is a woman; both are just human beings, potential gods, seeds of godliness.

Neither love alone can do it – because it is too much trouble – nor meditation alone can do it, because without love, meditation becomes more like the silence of a cemetery, of a graveyard. It is no longer dancing, it is no longer flowering. Yes, there is peace, but the peace is deathlike – it is not alive. The peace is no longer breathing, the peace no longer has a heartbeat.

My whole life has been devoted to only one single program: how to bring love and meditation together – because only through that meeting a new humanity is possible. And only in the meeting of love and meditation, the duality of man and woman – the inequality of man and woman – disappears.

The women's liberation movement cannot deliver the goods. I am not directly concerned with women's liberation, I am concerned with the liberation of all – because if woman is not liberated, man is also not liberated. They are functioning with each other as the jailer and the jailed; they are in bondage to each other. Neither man is liberated, nor woman – both are living under a slavery imposed by each other in the hope that perhaps if they enslave the other, they will be free. But the other has its own ways of enslaving you.

Only in meditation, in silence, where love blossoms, there is – without any struggle, without any fight – a natural harmony, equality, a natural equilibrium. And when it is natural, it has a beauty of its own.

The Rebellious Spirit, (Session 29).

CHAPTER 16

Who Wants To Be A Man?

I thought You knew everything. I thought that's what being enlightened is about: knowing. But You don't know about women, and that they trust precisely because they know each other's heart. Women's hate for women is a male myth invented to keep women separate and powerless. Who wants to be a man? Osho, I am totally upset. How can You talk nonsense? My mind is having a fit and so is my heart. What to do?

You say, "I thought You knew everything." You are absolutely wrong – I know nothing.

If you have come here with this idea, you have come to a wrong person and to a wrong place. We celebrate ignorance! We destroy all kinds of knowledge. Our whole effort is to bring innocence back to you, the innocence you had before you were born. Zen people call it "the original face." Innocence is intrinsic, knowledge is given to you by the society, by the people around you, by the family. Innocence is yours: knowledge is always of others. The more knowledgeable you are, the less you are yourself.

Enlightenment has nothing to do with knowledge. It is freedom from knowledge, it is absolute transcendence of knowledge. It is going beyond knowing. (...) An enlightened person is one who has no barrier between him and existence. And knowledge is a barrier. Knowledge divides you from existence; it keeps you separate. Not knowing unites you. Love is a way of innocence. Innocence is a bridge: knowledge is a wall. Who has ever heard of knowledgeable people becoming enlightened? They are the farthest away from enlightenment. Enlightenment grows only in the soil of innocence.

Innocence means childlike wonder, awe. The enlightened person is one who is continuously wondering – because he knows nothing, so everything becomes again a mystery. When you know, things are demystified; when you don't know, they are re-mystified. The more you know, the less wonder is in your heart. The more you know, the less you feel the great experience of awe. You cannot say "Ah, This!" You cannot be ecstatic. The knowledgeable person is so burdened that he cannot dance, he cannot sing, he cannot love. For the knowledgeable there is no God, because God only means wonder, awe, mystery. That's why, as knowledge has grown in the world, God has become further and further away.

Friedrich Nietzsche could declare that God is dead because of his knowledgeability. He was certainly a great philosopher, and philosophy is bound to come to the conclusion that there is no God because God simply means the mysterious, the miraculous and knowledge reduces every miracle to ordinary laws; every mystery is reduced to formulas.

Ask the knowledgeable person, "What is love?" and he will say, "Nothing but chemistry, the attraction between male and female hormones. It is no more important than a magnet attracting iron pieces. It is the same as positive and negative electricity: man and woman are bio-electricity."

Then everything is destroyed. Then all love and all poetry and all music are reduced to nonsense. The lotus is reduced to the mud. The lotus certainly grows out of the mud, but the lotus is not the mud. It is not the sum total of its parts; it is more than the sum total of the parts. That more is God, that more is poetry, that more is love. But science has no place for the "more." Science reduces every phenomenon to a mechanical thing. And do you know what "science" means? "Science" means knowledge.

Religion is not knowledge; it is just the opposite of knowledge. It is poetry, it is love. It is basically absurd. Yes, you can say that I am talking nonsense. But that's the beauty of it.

You say, "I thought you knew everything." That is your thought – and I am not here to oblige everybody's thought. I cannot be according to your thoughts. I have more than one hundred thousand sannyasins; if I am to fulfill everybody's thought I will be absolutely torn apart, into millions of pieces. I cannot fulfill your ideas about me; that is your mistake. And it is not too late either – drop that idea if you want to be here with me....

You are here with a paradoxical person, with a person who is trying to convey something mysterious to you – not knowledge – who is trying to pour his experience of wonder and awe into your beings – it is more like wine than like knowledge – who is trying to make you intoxicated, who is trying to transform you into drunkards. Yes, for the rational person it will look like nonsense.

That's what one of the most important thinkers of the West, Arthur Koestler, has written about Zen. He calls it "all nonsense." If you look rationally, it is – but is reason the only way to approach reality? There are other ways, far deeper, far more intimate – not knowing is the most intimate.

I am not a man of knowledge, although I use words. I am not even a man of words.

"I am a man of few words. Will you or won't you?"

"Your apartment or mine?" said the chick.

"Look," he said, "if there's going to be a lot of discussion about it, let's forget the whole damn thing!"

I use words, but I am not a man of words. It is just out of sheer necessity, it is because of you that I have to use words, because you won't understand the wordless. I am waiting eagerly for the day when I will be able to drop words. I am utterly tired... because words can't convey that which I am and I have to go on trying to do something which is not possible.

Get ready soon, so that we can sit in silence and listen to the birds or to the wind in the trees. Just sitting silently doing nothing, the spring comes and the grass grows by itself. That is going to be my ultimate message and my final work on the earth.

You say, "I thought that's what being enlightened is about: knowing." You cannot think about enlightenment, and whatsoever you think is bound to be wrong. It has nothing to do with knowing; it is a state of being.

"But don't you know about women and that they trust precisely because they know each other's heart." I know about nothing. What to say about women? – I don't even know about men! So don't be worried about that. If you know what a woman is or what a man is, beware of your knowledge, because that is not real knowing; it is just opinion that you have gathered.

Yes, man has been propagating ideas against women; now women are propagating ideas against men. It is the same foolish thing! And we go on doing this: we go on moving from one extreme to another extreme.

Now you say, "Women's hate for women is a male myth invented to keep women separate and powerless." Man bas created many myths about women, but now the women are doing the same. They are creating myths about men which are as false as man's myths about women. But I am not here to decide which myth is right and which myth is wrong. I am not here to make you a propagandist for women or against women. My work consists in freeing you from man/woman duality.

And now you say, "Who wants to be a man?" If you really don't want to be a man you would not have written this. It is just like the ancient parable of the fox who was trying to reach the grapes and could not reach: the grapes were too high. She tried and tried, and failed again and again. Then she looked around – foxes are very cunning people – to see if anybody was watching, any journalist, any photographer. There was nobody, so she walked away. But a small hare was hiding in a bush. He said "Auntie, what happened?"

The fox puffed her chest up as big as she could and said, "Nothing. Those grapes are not worthwhile. They are not ripe yet – they are sour."

Why should you write, "Who wants to be a man?" Deep down somewhere you must be hankering to be a man. Every man wants to be a woman, every woman wants to be a man, for the simple reason that every man is both – man/woman – and every woman is both – woman/man. You are born out of the meeting of male and female energies: half of you belongs to your father and half of you belongs to your mother. You are a meeting of two polar opposites, two energies.

The only difference between man and woman is this, that the woman has the consciousness of a woman and the unconscious of a man, and the man has the consciousness of a man and the unconsciousness of a woman. But both are both.

That's why it is possible to be homosexuals, lesbians; otherwise it would be impossible. This phenomenon has been happening down the ages; it is nothing new. The reason is simple: the man is only half man and half woman; the woman part is hidden deep in the darkness. But the conscious part can become tired, and when the conscious part becomes tired the unconscious takes over. Hence he may have the body of a man, but he starts functioning like a woman. And the same happens to a lesbian: on the surface she is a woman, but deep down the unconscious male energy has taken possession. Things have become upside down. It will affect her physiology too.

There are a few lesbians here. Their physiology is bound to be affected by their psychology, because psychology and physiology are not two separate phenomena; they are joined together. Mind and body are not two; you are mindbody. So whatsoever happens in your physiology affects your psychology. That's why hormones can be given to you and your psychology can be changed. Now we know a man can be changed into a woman, a woman can be changed into a man.

And this is my observation: in the coming century millions of people will change their sex. That will be a new kind of freedom. Why remain confined to being a man your whole life when you can have both the worlds? If you can afford it you can change your sex. For a few years you remain a man and you look at the world from the male's viewpoint, and then you go for a simple operation and you are changed into a woman; now you can look at the world through the feminine eyes. And it is possible that a man may change many times. If the process becomes simpler, and it will become simpler – that's the whole work of science: to make things simpler and simpler – if the process becomes very simple, millions of people are bound to change.

It will release a great freedom in the world, but a great confusion also, a great chaos also. One day suddenly your husband comes home and he is a woman! Or your wife returns from a holiday and she is no longer a woman...

Because each is both, the desire to be the other is in everybody. It must be there and very insistently there. Hence you are writing, "Who wants to be a man?"

And you ask me, "Osho, I am totally upset." That's good! So I am succeeding! I want you to be completely uprooted, upset, disturbed. I want to create a chaos in you, because only out of chaos are stars born.

You say, "How can you talk nonsense?" What else? Sense cannot be talked... only nonsense is left. So I don't take it as a criticism – it is a compliment! Many many thanks to you. At least you are talking some sense!

You say, "My mind is having a fit and so is my heart. What to do?" I don't think anything can be done now. It is too late. You can't go back – I will haunt you! – you can only go ahead. Drop all these ideas that you are carrying within yourself, this antagonism about men. Drop all these ideas! I am neither for men nor for women. I am only for transcendence.

And don't take my jokes seriously! You are such fools that you can't even take jokes playfully. Another woman has written, "Osho, You have been talking too much against women. The other day You called them 'big-mouths, nothing else!' "Nobody else has felt offended. A joke is a joke! But why are you so touchy? Now this woman must have a big mouth. At least her husband must be telling her again and again, "You big mouth, shut up!" And now she comes here to hear something beautiful said about her, and I tell a joke... and again that big mouth comes in.

Don't take jokes seriously. In fact, don't take anything seriously. You miss the point if you start taking things seriously. Even scriptures have to be taken non-seriously; only then can you understand. Understanding has to be with a deep, relaxed, non-serious, playful attitude. When you become serious you become closed. When you are playful many things can happen because in playfulness is creativity. In playfulness you can innovate. But your ideas are continuously there; you can't put them aside.

Now nothing can be done. You are a sannyasin. Now, being a sannyasin means you are neither man nor woman. Finished – that game is finished!

Ah, This!, Chapter 4.

Part II

Interviews by Lia Paradiso

In early March 1987, Osho was interviewed by Lia Paradiso. He answered twenty-two questions over a period of four evenings. Questions 1, 2 and 3 were answered on March 8th. Questions 4, 7, 8, 17, 18 and 19 were answered on March 9th. Questions 5, 6, 20, 21 and 22 were answered on March 10th, and questions 9 through 16 were answered on March 11th.

Osho,

1. Why are there still so many women engaged in the feminist movement, though it has not led to an existential change or real freedom?

The feminist movement is not, in the real sense, revolutionary. It is only reaction – and reactions don't lead anywhere, except to frustration, failure. But so many women are still engaged in it because they don't have any alternative; and they have become more and more female chauvinists, so they don't want to listen to any alternative that can be given to them.

I can give them an alternative, but just because I am in the body of a man, they become deaf to it. They don't have the understanding that a man who is enlightened is neither male nor female. He has transcended all dualities; he is pure consciousness – and consciousness is neither.

The movement has gone in the wrong direction from the very beginning. It started by asking for equality. It should have, rather, asked for equal opportunity, because the very idea of equality is absurd. Man is man, and woman is woman: no one is inferior and nobody is superior, nor are they equal. They are simply different – not only different but polar opposites. Their polar "oppositeness" is the very cause of their attraction towards each other.

The feminist movement started trying to imitate men so that women could be equal to men. This is both psychologically and spiritually wrong. A woman has different qualities to develop. She is not just to be a carbon copy of man; she has to be her original self. Therefore, I say, they need equal opportunity to be different and to be their own selves. And the further away woman and man are from each other, the better is the possibility of their becoming complementaries in a harmonious, loving relationship.

2. Your having the physical body of a man hinders a certain kind of woman, like feminists, intellectuals etc., from listening to You, especially when You speak on women. You said that an enlightened one is beyond being man or woman, that you are neither a man, nor a woman. Can You talk more about this?

I am just consciousness.

The woman who is a feminist is just being reactionary – she is not intellectual. A little intelligence will show that man has been very ugly and disgusting in his behavior towards women, but that does not mean that now women have to be the same towards man. The past is past, and intelligence knows how to forgive and how to forget and create a new situation.

Just being against man is destructive to both man

and woman. They cannot survive as enemies; they can live a beautiful life only as friends. Man has done much wrong by trying to enslave woman, and women have been reacting to it by being bitchy in every possible way so they are not absolutely innocent. And the feminist movement unfortunately has fallen into the hands of that bitchy type of woman; it is not in the hands of enlightened consciousness.

3. At this particular moment in time, it seems for woman there is nowhere more to go. She has been a wife and dropped that; was into politics and came out of it frustrated; and has been fighting against everything old and rotten. Still she has reached nowhere. But just hearing the word "religion," she becomes very disturbed. Why?

Religion has been anti-life, and woman has represented – to the so-called religious people – life itself, because she was the source of love and the source of new life and new arrivals. She was the center of the home, and she was very dominant inside the home.

All husbands have been henpecked; and just to get free of all this slavery they revolted, in the name of religion, against life itself – because "life" was more or less synonymous with "wife." It was out of fear, because the woman has always been attractive to the man, which is natural. And the people who escaped from life out of fear started preaching that woman is the cause of all sin, and celibacy became the greatest virtue.

The woman was condemned as a symbol of this earthly life. To oppose her was a kind of worship of

God; it was because of celibacy that men were so afraid and obsessed – celibacy is nothing but repression of sex. They were condemning the woman just to protect their celibacy. All religions have been obsessed because of this repression. Deep down they were attracted – and this was one of the ways to fight with their own attraction. Hence it is very relevant that the feminists become very much disturbed by even hearing the word "religion." This is one cause....

Deeper than this is the second cause, and that is: woman has not been allowed to grow religiously; and that too is a basic need for her. She has been denied initiation by almost all religions; she has not been allowed to be educated in religious scriptures.

Even in a country like England they are still fighting about whether to give women initiation as priestesses in the churches or not. The Church of England is on the verge of splitting in two on this point – those who want to give them a chance, and those who are against it. But my own understanding is that women should refuse to be part of any religion that has been established by men. They should create their own religion, which will have a different flavor. All that they have to learn is to drop their jealousies. Just as ego is man's problem, jealousy is the woman's problem. The ego prevents a man from spiritual growth, and jealousy prevents the woman.

I really feel puzzled about why women should even ask to be priestesses in a church that is basically male-oriented. Even Jesus did not accept among his twelve apostles the three women who loved him the most – Mary Magdalene, his own mother, Mary, and another woman of the same name, Mary.

So why bother at all? And this will be a more dignified attitude, that women refuse: "We don't want to become priestesses in a religion where even God is a trinity but there is no woman in it." Women should create everything of their own, not as a reaction but just according to their nature, according to their own inclination, according to their own sensitivity; and this will create such a great revolution – because all the churches and temples are full of women! Only the bishop and the priest and the cardinal are men. So leave those churches! No woman should go to these churches.

When the Archbishop of Greece threatened that he would burn and dynamite the house where I was staying if I didn't leave at once, and the government became afraid and I was immediately arrested without any reason, I inquired, "How many people has he got in his church?" There were only six old women – that was his whole congregation!

Woman has been fighting to be a priest, to be a politician... and finds herself in frustration. The real thing will be when she boycotts all politics that are man -created; when she makes it a point that the whole earth is one – she is half of the population – when she starts denying all demarcations of nation, of religion, of color, of race. That will not only help her, that will help man too. But up to now, whatever she has done has been just imitating man. Woman needs real rebellious ideology.

Women should simply leave all these man-made, anti-woman institutions – they have enough power and great enough numbers to create their own world.

And they have to remember one thing, that in

nature woman is much more of a necessity than man. The man's function in reproduction is almost nil. It can be done by an injection, a syringe.

Woman can be absolutely free of man.

Rather than being beggars – "Give us initiation, give us this, give us that" – women should declare, "We are liberated," and men will be in the position of begging. And that will be far better; then women can give to men. But asking men to give things is very difficult because they have centuries of past behind them, and they cannot accept anything that goes against the tradition.

The woman has to start afresh – a new world of her own, in which, out of love and compassion, she can accept man.

For example, she should start denying marriage – she should stand for love. On the contrary, she is becoming lesbian, which is absolutely ugly and unnatural. And when birth control methods are available, there is no question of being worried about having children. She should insist on living with man without marriage. She should make women's communes in every society, in every city; and all the children that are born should belong to the commune. In this way she will be out of the grip of the family.

Woman should move in directions which are natural to her. For example, rather than be a politician, she should be a dancer, a singer, an actor, a poet, a painter and... other crafts. She should put all her energy and genius into those dimensions which are natural to her. And she has such huge support all over the world from all the women and all the men who have any understanding of human nature, that she will create her own Nobel prizes, she will create her own universities. She should insist that she has an individuality of her own, and she should train for that individuality: she should make society pay respect to the dimensions in which she is working.

She should not participate in any kind of war, and she should try to prevent her lovers, her children... persuade them to be anti-war, anti-destruction. She should also prevent them from being anti-life, from being monks and nuns. She has to create a whole philosophy of life-affirmation which will destroy all these religions automatically, and it will give her a chance to develop her own religious potential.

And there is no problem as far as enlightenment is concerned: woman is as capable as man and the methods are so scientific that they are nobody's monopoly.

But just getting disturbed by the word "religion" is not going to help.

4. In the past, in the East, women were respected and allowed to argue with the so-called wise men, even in court; but in the West it has never been so. Is there any particular reason why this difference was there?

This was in the very early days of civilization in the East, that is, five thousand years ago, when marriage had not yet become settled and the society was changing from being a hunting society to an agricultural one.

In a hunting society there was no marriage; marriage

came into existence when society became a cultivating society; with cultivation there was land, possessions, and the idea of man that his own sons should inherit his land. So, in fact, marriage came as a by-product of private ownership. That was the only way to be certain that your son is yours – that the woman is monogamous. Those stories of the ancient days are of the days of those thousands of years of transition from hunting to agriculture. Once agriculture became established, woman lost freedom in the East too.

The East became civilized almost three thousand years earlier than the West. When the East was at its peak of civilization, the West was still at the hunting stage. And geographical differences – the cold in the West – made the woman more dependent on man than in the warmer countries. Life in the West was harder; it was much more of a struggle to survive.

It is a strange fate that the West moved all over the East for the simple reason that because of the hardship of their lives, the Westerners have become better fighters; and the East – because of a good climate, rich land and comfortable life – made people weaker, they were not ready to fight. India has never invaded any country, and it has been invaded by almost every country. Even very barbarous tribes, minority groups, were able to capture and rule India. People were so comfortable that they did not want to fight: "If you want to rule, you rule."

Man in the West became very strong because he was the warrior; and the woman became weaker and more dependent.

In Europe the transition period from hunting to

agriculture was almost nil, and the reason was that in the East agriculture had become absolutely established five thousand years earlier, so everything about agriculture was available to the West. Because the transition period was very short, it never gave any chance for a loose and changing atmosphere in which nothing was settled, and the woman did not have the same opportunity as she did in the East.

It is almost parallel to the situation now. In the West, the scientific revolution happened three hundred years ago, and for three hundred years there has been a constant fight between the church and science. Only now has the church accepted that there is no way to prevent science, and the struggle has ceased. In the East there has been no evolution of science in these three hundred years, but whatever has developed in the West is now transferred to the East – the whole technology.

That's why, in the East, there is no fight between religion and science. In the beginning the church was powerful, and scientists were individuals – they could be crushed. But slowly slowly, scientists became more and more powerful because what they were doing was objectively true and immensely beneficial to humanity. But it took three hundred years for the church to understand this situation – that it was fighting a losing battle. In the East there has been no fight at all, because the whole of science is borrowed, and it is borrowed in a very developed form.

Exactly the same happened with agriculture: it became established in the East, but it took time to become established, and the West borrowed agriculture from the East.

5. In ancient times in Egypt and other countries, there were high priestesses. Why today do we only have popes?

In fact, the ancient cultures were not intellectual cultures, they were more intuitive, and woman is far superior in intuition; hence there were high priestesses, but no popes.

Now the situation is completely reversed. Science is totally intellectual, philosophy is intellectual, and the organized religions are intellectual. Those priestesses were individuals; they had no organized religion, because on the basis of intuition you cannot organize a religion. These intellectually-organized religions are man-dominated, so they will have popes. Also, they have destroyed all the remnants of old cultures and their priestesses, calling them witches.

One thing more: there was a similar phenomenon with these priestesses in Egypt and in India. Not only in the past, but even today there are remnants of it. In many parts of India, particularly the south, it is a tradition that every family gives their first daughter to the temple. These girls are called devadasis, "in the service of God." They work as priestesses and they also work as prostitutes.

To go to an ordinary prostitute looks awkward to people, but to go to a temple prostitute is thought to be something religious, as if she is transforming and transmitting some divine energy – and this is an absolute fiction. So there are thousands of women still, even today, attached to temples. Those temples get the money, and the women function as prostitutes. The

Indian constitution has made it illegal, but has not been able to stop it. So even when there were priestesses in the temple, man took advantage of that: the women were turned into spiritual prostitutes.

6. What is a witch? Is the witch the same as the "new man" that You talk about?

"Witch" is a very respectable word which Christianity has condemned. Originally it simply meant "the wise woman," but Christianity gave it a very distorted meaning because, according to it, the devil corrupted the mind of Eve first, and since then he has been in conspiracy with woman. So she cannot be wise because her wisdom is not from God, it is from the devil. Once they had given it this meaning, then the door was open to condemn the woman more. And there were women who were really wise, particularly in the school of the alchemists – that is one of the branches of mysticism.

These alchemist women were, in the eyes of the Christian priests, their competitors, and they had to be destroyed. To destroy them they had to find a certain rationalization, and this was their reasoning: that these women were having sexual intercourse with the devil. A special court was appointed by the pope, with a "Grand Inquisitor," whose whole work was to find out all the witches and burn them – alive. And the method that was used to find them was: any man could report to the court that he suspected a certain woman was a witch – this was enough to arrest the woman.

They invented certain methods of torturing her, and the torture was so ugly that it was almost impossible for the woman to tolerate. And unless she confessed that she had been having intercourse with the devil, the torture continued for weeks on end. Once she had confessed, then she had to confess it before the Grand Inquisition court, which consisted of cardinals and archbishops and high-ranking Christian priests. And they forced these women not only to confess that they had been having intercourse with the devil, they were even forced to tell the court that the devil's penis was forked so that it could enter the woman from both places together. This was enough for the court to burn these women alive. So absolutely innocent women, in thousands, were burned alive.

The basic reason was that they were far wiser than the Christian priests, and they had to be eliminated completely so no competition remained.

And I will not say that the future man is going to be a witch: the witch is as much a part of the past as the priest. The new man will not have priests – man or woman – as mediators between himself and existence; his contact with existence will be immediate and individual. There is no possibility of any organized religion in the future.

7. Should there be a different meditation technique for men and women?

No, because meditation is concerned with consciousness – which is neither male nor female.

8. What is the difference between female energy and male energy, and can both be

contained in the same body? How to find a harmonious way to deal with this issue?

The difference between male and female energy is exactly that of electricity. The male energy is positive bio-electricity, and the female is negative bio-electricity – and in each body both energies are available. If the positive is more powerful, the body is that of a man; if the negative is more powerful, then the body is that of a woman. But because every child is born out of a man and a woman, it naturally carries both the energies. Because of this possibility, through plastic surgery, sex can be converted.

In the science of Tantra there are meditations in which both the energies in the same body can have a merging and a meeting. That meeting of man and woman in one body brings transcendence – then the outer body may remain a man or a woman's, but the inner being is no longer divided, it becomes an organic unity. And the problem of how to harmonize them is absolutely man-created.

Both man and woman are polygamous, so any relationship soon becomes boring. A more mobile society is needed where sex is not to be taken seriously, but more playfully, as fun. And now, because of the pill, this is possible. According to me, the pill is the greatest revolution in human history because it can change the whole structure of human relationships.

9. There are many different causes which bring two people of the opposite sex together. One of them is a physical attraction, which

is basically caused by chemical hormones; or a deeper one, which can be the woman's search for a father-figure, or the man's search for a mother-figure. For whatever reasons the choice of one's partner is made, it is unconscious. Is this perhaps one of the reasons why a healthy relationship between a woman and a man is almost impossible?

Yes, it is one of the most significant reasons for unhappy relationships between man and woman.

This can be destroyed only if children are brought up by the commune, and not by a family – because in the family the girl has only the father to get a fixation on, and the boy has only the mother. These father and mother fixations grow from the very beginning so they go very deep; and later on, when one falls in love, these fixations are the determining factors. The girl is searching for a father, and the boy is searching for a mother. They fall in love because something in both seems to be similar. But as they get married and start living together and become more acquainted, they find that they have been deluded – because no woman can be exactly like the boy's mother nor can a man prove to be exactly like the girl's father.

Secondly – this is the unconscious desire – the conscious desire of the woman is to find a lover, and of the boy to find a beloved. So neither the girl wants to be the mother nor the boy wants to be the father, so their conscious and their unconscious come into conflict. It becomes an inner turmoil which they project on each other.

But if the child is brought up in a commune, where the boy will come in contact with many women and the girl will come in contact with many men, they will not have a fixed image of a father or mother, but only a vague image of man and woman. Those vague figures can fit with each other.

Thirdly: children should be allowed to play sexually – that is the real education. By the age when girls can become pregnant, they should have made love to many boys, and boys should have made love to many girls. And as they become of the age when the girls can become pregnant, it is the responsibility of the commune to provide them with adequate means so they can go on playing with sex without any fear. If a girl has made love to many men and then decides upon one man – and the same is true about the man – there is more possibility of harmonious relations. Their decision will be out of understanding, maturity, and much experience. Right now it is a very blind game. Both are inexperienced, and suddenly they decide that they want to be together. It is destined to fail.

And if my ideas are followed, jealousy will disappear completely because the girls have known so many men, and the men have known so many girls, so the very question of monopoly, possessiveness and jealousy is bound to disappear.

And still it has to be remembered that nobody gets married – because it is none of the business of law or society; it is two persons' individual affair. That will prevent couples being hypocrites and insincere about each other, because whenever they feel that their love is no longer there they can separate joyously, as friends, with beautiful memories of the past, no complaints, no grudge.

It has to be made a fundamental understanding that love is not a permanent thing, that like anything alive, it changes, so nobody is to be blamed. Up to now the poets particularly have been giving the idea to humanity that love is something permanent, and if it is not permanent then it is not true love. But I want to make it clear that only untrue love can be permanent; true love can never be permanent. It comes like the spring and it goes, and there is no need to cry over the spilt milk. One starts finding another partner.

The more lovers you have in your life, the richer will be your experience, because no two women or two men are the same. And it is good that people go on changing – getting stuck with one person is the cause of much misery. And once love is not there, to go on living with the person is nothing but prostitution....

10. Most of the time, giving birth to a child is not out of our own choice, but a mere instinct for reproduction. One of the most mysterious relationships is between a woman and a child. Can You speak about the womb relationship? Considering that most of the time this relationship is based on an old conditioning like possessiveness, how can a woman avoid that and help the child to grow without cutting its wings?

In the old times it was one thing, but now the whole situation is different; having a child has to be a conscious choice. In the past, it was simply instinctive, but now it can be a totally different phenomenon.

According to me, a child should not be born between two lovers... because in each ejaculation at least a million sperms are released, and only one reaches the woman's egg. There is tremendous competition: all those millions of sperms are rushing towards the egg. To us their journey is small, but to them, in proportion to their size, it is almost two miles long. And there is every possibility that the best ones will not be the winners, but the stronger ones will reach first. So we don't know how many geniuses we go on missing – because their sperms' life span is only two hours.

The scientific thing would be for every hospital to have a sperm bank, just like a blood bank, and a couple can have an absolutely definite choice about what kind of child they want. The whole potential of life is contained in a sperm; and now it has become possible to read in it what this sperm will become in the future – an Albert Einstein, a Kahlil Gibran, a Friedrich Nietzsche, or an Adolf Hitler. We can avoid all the wrong kinds of people who there was no way to avoid in the past.

We can avoid children who will be blind, children who will be retarded, children who will be crippled, children who will die soon, children who will suffer their whole life from weakness and diseases.

We can choose the musician, the mathematician, the scientist, the poet, the philosopher, the mystic. This will make such a tremendous revolution that the world can be immensely rich. And the sperm should be provided by the hospital and injected into the woman, so from the very beginning the idea of possessiveness is cut. The child is coming through you, but it is not yours. This is getting out of the imprisonment of biology.

And secondly, it makes sex fun – because out of sexual intercourse children should not be produced at all. Then the relationship between the mother and the child will automatically go through a change. The father is unknown and the mother has only provided her womb; the child belongs to the commune. There can only be a loving relationship, but possessiveness is out of the question. The possessive arises out of the upbringing of the child in the family.

And this is only for the present; within just a few years the possibility will be available that eggs from the mothers can also have a bank in the hospital, and the womb can be mechanical. It will look inhuman in the beginning but it will create a far better human society.

11. Can giving birth to a child for a woman on the path of meditation be only a hindrance, or is there a particular instance when it will help her and her spiritual growth?

It is always going to be a hindrance.

12. Many men – for example, Buddha – left their family in search of enlightenment. Has it ever happened that an enlightened being started a family after enlightenment?

No, it has never happened, and it will never happen, for the simple reason that a family will be a hindrance for the enlightened person in creating a commune –

that is his real family. So he can give his love, his care to the disciples – a family will cause unnecessary trouble.

13. You once said that it is possible in the future that an enlightened child is born; but at another time You said that no enlightened being ever comes back into the womb. Please comment.

It is true that the enlightened being never comes back into the womb. But there is a possibility that somebody who was just going to be enlightened, dies: he will be born almost enlightened, and without much effort he will become enlightened. But a fully enlightened person cannot enter into a womb.

14. Even when intellectually accepted, abortion is a difficult task for a woman. Why?

In fact there should be no need for abortion. Now, three kinds of pills are available. Before there was only one kind of pill, and if you had missed taking it before making love, just by accident you could get pregnant. Now another kind of pill has just been marketed – that can be taken after making love. And a third pill has also become available – that can be taken by the man. So if a little intelligence is there, there is no need for abortion.

Abortion is basically ugly – it was a necessary evil – because you are destroying life. It is inhuman, cruel, and against life. There should be a reverence for life.

So abortion will soon be a thing of the past.

15. Birth-control education seems to have failed, particularly in Third-World countries, thanks to the popes, acharyas and all the saints. The world is overpopulating fast. How can woman be educated about this in spite of the strong biological urge to create children, the irresponsible enforcing of this and the conditioning from the traditional religions?

First: it is not so much the biological urge. I know the poorest women of the East who are absolutely exhausted and tired of children because they are constantly pregnant. It is a torture.

There is a biological urge to make love, but not to get pregnant. It is the religions who are solely responsible, who go on forcing the idea that birth-control methods are against God. The women can be convinced to use them but no effort has been made. The politicians are afraid to annoy the religions, and there is nobody else to convince the woman. It should be part of the women's liberation movement to convince them, and I don't think that they will be resistant to it.

The fight has to be against the religious heads – and an active movement should be started. For example, wherever the Pope goes, women should protest against him and make every effort to prevent his entry into any country; women should even try to take over the Vatican. And the same should be done against the others – the Shankaracharyas, the Ayatollah Khomeinis.... In every church, in any temple, on any holiday, there should be a protest – it should be a continuous struggle.

And I think it can succeed because even many men will help in it. So active support should be invited from men too – that these so-called religious heads have to be silenced; otherwise, they are going to destroy humanity without any nuclear bombs.

16. Why have women never thought about war?

First: woman does not have a war instinct, and she is not interested in invading countries, creating empires. It is just not in her nature. That's why I'm insisting that if women took over all the parliaments, war could simply be stopped without any difficulty.

It is the woman who suffers most in a war: either her husband dies or her son dies or her father dies. Whenever her country is invaded, the first victim is the woman. She is raped by the soldiers of the invading nation; the first thing that the soldiers do is to rape women. She gets nothing out of war except losing everything and being used brutally and violently.

War will continue if man remains in power. Man has to be removed from power – he has a war instinct.

17. Women had to struggle hard to become equal to men, succeeding in many fields of science, medicine and literature. But still, in spite of the success, the failure has been bigger – still the emptiness remains. Can this be a good stepping-stone for meditation?

It is.

The very effort was bound to fail because it was not coming out of spontaneity, it was a competition with men. Once we give equal opportunity to both to be different, and it is understood that there is no question of equality – they are different and unique – then more spontaneous efforts will create novels, painting, poetry, music. There will be no question of competition with anyone. Anything that arises as a competition is out of tension, antagonism, and it cannot be of a very superior order.

So the first thing is to change the political structure in the world – then, make women economically free from men. That can be the second step, and that can only be the second step: unless women are in power, you cannot make them free. In the past man has destroyed woman by a simple strategy: making her financially dependent on him. Even if a woman lives with a man, she has to remain financially independent.

The feminist movement has almost failed.

I suggest that women create an international women's party, and that they demand a separate vote in every country.

By separate vote, I mean women will vote only for women, and men will vote only for men. That will change the whole structure of all the parliaments in the world, because half of the members of parliament will be women, and half, men. The men will be divided into political parties, but the women will not be divided into any parties; they will be one party, a single party. In this way they can take over the world without any difficulty. So this has to be the struggle for the future.

And it should be made compulsory that no woman can vote for a man, and no man can vote for a woman. That can create immediately a great upheaval all around the world. Once women are in power all over the world, they can start changing the bureaucracy that man has created; they can start destroying the nuclear weapons; they can start making all educational systems not only man-oriented. Half the bureaucracy should be handed over to women, and that should be the rule in other fields also: half the students in medical colleges should be women. Whatever the proportion of the women in the country – that should be the proportion in all the fields that suit them. Half the professors in the universities....

And there may be a few fields where women may do better: then they should be given one hundred percent to women. And a few things that men can do better should be given one hundred percent to men. So again it should be remembered: equal opportunity, not equality.

18. Women like Simone de Beauvoir, Virginia Woolf, Gertrude Stein, Vita Sackville West, Lou Andreas Salome, Sophia Loren or any of the women of this century that You know – could they have become enlightened with a master?

Women have the same capacity to become enlightened as men. The number will be almost equal, because nature keeps a certain balance – for example, Gertrude Stein certainly could have become enlightened.

Enlightenment is not the monopoly of man – but he has made it a monopoly in the past. All these monopolies can be destroyed. One thing has to be understood very clearly: without changing the political structure, nothing can be changed.

And women should not get divided into parties; otherwise they will be crushed, they will not be able to do anything. Their whole ideology should be for the liberation of women, and for creating equal opportunity in all fields. And the struggle should be world-wide, so in every nation.... Unless the struggle is world-wide, it will be very difficult to change the whole structure.

And it is such a simple thing to create a world revolution. It is far simpler than it was for the proletariat to create a world revolution, because they fell into the same trap: there were so many small parties with minor differences in China, the Soviet Union, Yugoslavia and other communist parties.

So there should be a basic ideology, emphasizing simply that the woman has to take over the world.

19. But will there not be a disparity in different women in different parts of the world as far as their being ready to take economic freedom from man and set up their own political parties? For example, are the women in India ready for such a move?

We should try. Wherever it can happen, it should happen; the idea should be of a world revolution. It will take a few years because history takes strange detours.

Marx had never thought that communism would come to Russia or to China. He was thinking communism would happen first in America. Russia was very backward but conditions after the second world war helped; the soldiers revolted against the Czar, and communists took advantage of the situation. It was not really a communist revolution.

China was a very poor country: nobody could have thought that there would be a possibility of communism, but it happened because the background was Buddhism. In India it has not been possible. The communist party in India is as old as Russian communism – the Chinese communist party is a very new phenomenon – but in India the situation was different. Hinduism has conditioned people's minds for centuries that it is God who decides when you are to be poor or to be rich; it has nothing to do with the social structure.

So nobody can predict... but we should make it a point that we can think of the whole world. And women should move as missionaries around the world, spreading the idea, "We need a separate vote." And the idea is so simple that it cannot be denied, but by that simple idea the whole thing can be changed.

So it may happen in the West first, it may happen in the East – nothing can be said about it. Just one thing has to be remembered: it should not fall into divisions – which has been preventing communism from becoming a world revolution.

20. Does woman's real revolution still need to happen?

Yes, it still needs to happen. Up to now what has happened is only a reaction, and a reaction never liberates anyone because it is tied to the action. The moment there is no action, the reaction becomes meaningless.

A revolution has to be something beyond action and reaction – not out of anger, not out of hate, but out of understanding. The women's liberation movement, up to now, has not been out of understanding. Still, it is good that it has happened: it has prepared the ground for the real revolution.

21. It is said that behind every great man there is a woman. Is that so? Who is the woman behind You?

The proverb is just a consolation to women – it is not correct.

As far as I am concerned personally, there is no woman behind me. Collectively there are thousands of women behind me, but they are not the cause of my enlightenment; they are the effect. They came to me after my experience happened.

22. Has there ever been any enlightened master answering questions about the evolution of the state of women in regard to male domination?, an enlightened master speaking of a change in social rules and the future path to follow?

No, there has never been any enlightened master who was concerned about women and their evolution. They all remained confined to men for a simple reason – because they all emphasized that celibacy is the foundation of spiritual growth. It was a fallacy; and because of celibacy they were afraid of giving initiation to women or helping them with their evolution. The fear was about their male disciples – that they might get lost in sexual relationships with women and forget about their spiritual growth completely.

Nor has any enlightened master ever talked about changes in the social structure, revolutions in the economic divisions, revolts against different kinds of classes, exploitation, oppression, slavery. They simply kept themselves away from any concern for society. It was thought that it was not their business: they had renounced society, and they had nothing to do with it any more.

It was, in a way, a safety and security for themselves and for their disciples, because the establishment in the society was always very respectful to these people. The rich, the powerful, the kings, the politicians – they were all immensely happy that these geniuses were completely ignoring what was happening in the society. That was in their own interests, and they paid enlightened ones tremendous respect as a reward.

I have been advised by many well-wishing sages and saints that I should keep myself confined only to the spiritual dimension; otherwise I will be condemned by all those who are powerful. And that has actually been happening. They are not assassinating me out of the fear that my assassination may create more sympathy and understanding in the masses about me. It may also crystallize my disciples into a force. And this has been actually accepted by the Attorney General of America, Mr. Meese.

In a press conference he was asked, "Why was Osho not jailed?" And he said, "There are three reasons. First:

our priority was to destroy the commune. Second: we did not want Osho to become a martyr. And third: we had no evidence of any crime that he has committed." And this is the same man who produced before the court thirty-six crimes committed by me!

During the twelve days that I was in their jails, they moved me from one jail to another just to harass me, and every jailer who was delivering me to another jailer, whispered in his ear – which I could hear because I was standing just by his side – "This man is a world figure so don't do anything directly to him; anything indirectly is okay." And they tried on three occasions to kill me – but in an indirect way.

One jail they took me to, but not under my own name, and they forced me... if I wanted to sleep at all that night – it was the middle of the night – then I would have to sign the name "David Washington." It was the jail of Oklahoma. I told the jailer, "Any idiot can understand what the reason behind this is: you can simply kill me, and there will be no trace at all that I ever entered your jail and nobody will ever suspect that I was David Washington."

But the situation was saved because there was one woman prisoner who was going to be released. She was also present outside the cell where this whole dialogue was happening – when I was refusing to sign – and she heard the whole thing.

I told the jailer, "You fill in the whole form, and I will sign." My reasoning was simple, that his writing would be there and I would sign my signature – which is world famous – everyone would know whose signature it was. And as I came out, I told the woman: "You have heard everything. You are being released: just outside, there will be hundreds of reporters and news media people – inform them of what you have heard." So just the next morning in all the papers and on the television, the news was all over America, and at seven o'clock they immediately moved me from that jail.

In twelve days they took me to five jails, without any reason. From where they arrested me in North Carolina – without any arrest warrant, without showing any cause, without allowing me any contact with my attorney, which is my legal right – the distance to Portland, Oregon, is only five hours by air. I had to take twelve days to cover those five hours. They were perfectly aware that once I was produced before a judge I would be released, so whatever they were going to do, they had to do before I was in front of the judge.

In another jail they put me with a confirmed case of herpes – a man who was going to die just within a week at the most. For six months they had not put anybody else in that cell because the doctor wouldn't allow it; but when I was put in the cell, the doctor was present, the jailer was present, the U.S. marshal was present. As they left, the man – the prisoner who was dying – told me, "Osho, I don't know you, but I have been seeing you on the television and I have fallen in love with you. I am going to die, but I don't want you to catch the infection – and this room is completely infected, I have been there for six months. So don't you move from inside the door' just remain by the door, and don't touch anything. Knock on the door – it will take one or two or three hours for them to come."

Just two or three cells away was the office, but he was right: it took almost two hours for them to appear, and as I spoke to them, they became afraid. I told them, "I will give this report to the news media – the whole world will know." Immediately I was transferred to another cell. And the day I left the jail in Portland, a bomb was found under my chair.

So they tried their best to somehow kill me but not to take the responsibility on themselves. And now almost one year has passed but they are continuously trying to set every government in the world against me. And there is every possibility that they may have hired some professional killers so the responsibility does not fall on America... because this information about professional killers has come from a very top FBI officer who is a friend of a sannyasin. And in this life it does not seem to be improbable....

It has been found just now that when Ronald Reagan bombed Libya without any reason at all, it was just a strategy so that the whole attention of Libya and the world became focused on the bombs – and the professional killers could murder Gadaffi. Now this has been revealed to the American Senate.

In the past no enlightened master has dared to take the risk of losing respectability and being condemned. But to me respectability means nothing. The unconscious masses and their respectability has no meaning at all. Even if it means death to me, I am going to say everything that can bring the new man and the new humanity into existence.

FULL CIRCLE

Full Circle is a distinguished publisher of non-fiction, and classic and contemporary fiction. Known for quality publishing and production, Full Circle continues its commitment towards providing good reading at great value.

We are dedicated towards creating a peaceful and harmonious inner and outer world ever mindful of our connection with the divine human spirit.

Our fine books are available at leading bookstores across the country and the Full Circle Bookstores below:

Bookstores

23, Khan Market, 1st & 2nd Floor
New Delhi-110003 Tel: 24655641/2/3

N-16, Greater Kailash Part I Market
New Delhi-110048 Tel: 29245641/2/3/4

Number 8, Nizamuddin East Market
New Delhi-110013 Tel: 41826124/5

Editorial Office

J-40, Jorbagh Lane, New Delhi-110003
Tel: +011-24621011

contact@fullcirclebooks.in • www.fullcirclebooks.in